GROWING UP IN MISSION

Ex Libris

Lowell R. Kantzer

GROWING UP

A Leader's Handbook on the Education of

IN MISSION

Children in the Mission of the Church

by Grace Storms Tower

FRIENDSHIP   PRESS
New York

LIBRARY OF CONGRESS CATALOG CARD NUMBER: 66-11123

For
SCOTT, COURTNEY, GRAHAM, and MARC
and all children—heirs of the mission

CONTENTS

PART I

"Go therefore and make disciples . . ."

PART II

"You shall be my witnesses . . ."

PART III

"He took them in his arms . . ."

PART IV

"First the blade . . ."

GROWING UP IN MISSION

PART I

"Go therefore and make disciples . . ."

Go therefore and make disciples
of all nations . . . and lo, I am with
you always, to the close of the age.
Matthew 28:19a, 20b

An Introduction: The Old Order and the New

A generation or two ago we studied *missionary* education—a term which had a clear-cut meaning for leaders of children in the church. It involved teaching children about mission work around the world, about the great missionary leaders of the church, and about the ways boys and girls could help to support and participate in the mission program.

In more recent times *missionary* education for children placed a strong emphasis on world friendship. This, too, was definite in goal and content. Children were encouraged to respect and care for other people, to be interested in the work of the church around the world, and to want to help the church help others.

Today, however, *missionary* education has evolved into *mission* education—a term which is not nearly as specific in content and purpose. There are reasons for this change, ranging from developments on the international scene to the church's own efforts to understand more clearly what God is calling it to do.

Some of these developments may seem at first glance to threaten the very foundations of the church's missionary concern. For example, the rising tide of nationalism has led people in a number of countries to try to disassociate themselves from all "foreign" influences. Because the Christian church has been identified with the West, and in some situations with Western imperialism and colonialism, several of these countries have outlawed all Christian work which has conversion as its goal. At the same time, other world religions have been initiating active mission programs of their own in the United States and elsewhere. There are now Hindu and Buddhist missionaries busily at work making converts in North America.

Another development that challenges the missionary activity of the church and some popular concepts of missionary education is the radical change in life created by scientific achievement. The peoples of the earth are now joined together by mass communication, rapid transportation, advances in space research and in modern medicine—all of which are made possible through scientific research and discovery. People are aware of how important science is in their everyday lives. They are also aware of the military weapons science has produced for war, and the protection science professes to offer against these weapons. "In science we trust" is a significant twentieth century attitude.

Still another development is the population explosion at home and abroad. Fantastic forecasts have been made for the world's population by the year 2000 if the present trend in population growth continues. Political ideologies and religious faiths are battling for the control of the world's population. Today, when the Christian compares his numerical strength with that of communism and some of the other major world religions, he recognizes how much in the minority he is.

There are still other developments which affect the life of the church and the vigor of some aspects of the missionary enterprise. Among these are the secular spirit which stresses success, prosperity, and status as primary values; the growth of urban centers with a resulting breakdown in community relationships and moral control; the general prosperity of the West and the availability of material comforts; the feeling of helplessness expressed by many who think they have no control over their own future and the future of the human race; the inability of persons to live as neighbors because of racial, cultural, and religious differences. These cannot be ignored by anyone who would understand the human scene in which the mission of the church is carried on. Thoughtful Christians everywhere are wondering: How does the church witness to people who are involved in this kind of a world and in this kind of a culture?

This may seem to be a grim picture, and it is. Yet in the midst of this darkness there is light, and changes and developments on the mission scene give evidences of this light.

Today the church, aware that it has a message people desperately need to hear, is seeking ways to communicate this message so that all persons will reach out toward the loving God who is reaching out to them. And this very seeking has led the church to question many of its traditional concepts and practices.

In the past, the church has sometimes sought answers to its most central questions about its own nature and mission in authorities outside its own life. A very significant development in the current searching for new effectiveness is the returning of churchmen to the Bible, to God's self-revelation in the record of biblical events and experiences.

Serious Bible study has brought a renewed awareness of what God has promised to his people, a certainty that the security of the Christian is not found in human power, in the marvels of science, but in the sureness of God's love and God's faithfulness.

From this Bible study has come a deepening conviction that God is active in present-day events just as he was active in the history of the Hebrew people and the early Christians.

From this Bible study has come the understanding that the Christian community nurtures its own life and faith in order to be an effective representative of God in the community outside the church.

From this Bible study has come an awakened sense that all members of the Christian church are important in its life and work. It is not the professional missionary or the minister alone who does what the church is in existence to accomplish. The total fellowship is charged by God with this task.

From this Bible study has come the concept of *the church as mission,* established in the world by God to make his saving love known to all. The church is a fellowship that tests itself not by the success of its program but by the effectiveness of its witness.

These insights, growing out of an earnest attempt to grasp what God is saying to his people in the Bible, are making a difference in the life and mission of the church and inevitably in the church's program of *mission* education. This difference is reaching into the children's division. It is creating changes in what is done. It is influencing the motivation for mission, the materials that are published, the nature of the programs that are recommended, even the vocabulary that is used.

The history of *missionary* education indicates that originally its purpose was to recruit and support missionaries for service on the foreign and home mission frontiers. The purpose of *mission* education today is very close to this historic goal. But there is a difference. Today the church is aware that everyone who claims relationship to Jesus Christ as his Lord is a missionary because he must be about the mission of the church. He must be engaged in the business of witnessing to others what God has done for him and for all men in Christ. This is the biblical concept of mission.

Children of the church participate in this mission. In the pages that follow is some guidance for adults who want to help children understand what this mission is and how children may live and act as God's representatives in the world in which they live.

1: The Mission of the Church

A layman called on a minister to suggest that a woman in the community be involved in the church. The layman explained, "She's old and rich and lonely. She needs something to do, and if you get her now, there's a good chance she'll put the church in her will."

A neighbor overheard a fifth-grade boy talking to a school friend about family activities on Sunday morning. Apparently the school friend was not attending any church. As the two were separating, the fifth-grader urged, "Come to my church next Sunday. You can be in my class."

In the first situation, a well-meaning and interested member of a local church tried to help his minister help the church. The layman may also have had the needs of the elderly woman in mind. But is there not something wrong with the layman's suggestion?

In the second situation, a boy is communicating his enthusiasm about Sunday church school to his friend and trying to involve the friend in what has genuine meaning for the boy.

In the second situation, two elements are present that are absent in the first. The layman gives no indication that he is interested in sharing with the woman any meaning the church may hold for

him. The layman does not reveal any concern for the woman as a
person. The second situation has much more of the biblical motivation for mission than the first, even though the star in the drama
is a youngster and the setting a family yard.

With these two illustrations in mind, let us examine what we
mean when we talk about the mission of the church or the church
as mission.

WHAT IS MISSION?

The word "mission" is related to a Latin word meaning "to
send." Ever since its beginning, mission has been central in the
church's life. In fact, the Bible makes it clear that the church
exists to perform a distinctive kind of mission: to send out persons
to proclaim the good news of God's saving love to mankind.

In the first chapter of the book of Acts, there is a very interesting account of the setting in which this mission began. The time
is the post-resurrection period. Jesus and his followers are talking,
and it is evident that the disciples are still hoping for earthly political power. When Jesus reaffirms his promise that they will be baptized with the Holy Spirit, the disciples respond, "Lord, will you
at this time restore the Kingdom to Israel?"

In his answer, Jesus reminds the disciples of who they are and
the great task that is theirs to do, a task that cannot be confined
within any political goal. ". . . and you shall be my witnesses in
Jerusalem and in all Judea and Samaria and to the end of the
earth." (Acts 1:8b)

A short time later, when the group had assembled somewhere in
the city of Jerusalem, the Holy Spirit did come, the church was
created by God, and Peter immediately witnessed to puzzled on-
lookers about the meaning of what he had seen and heard. "Let
all the house of Israel therefore know assuredly that God has made
him both Lord and Christ, this Jesus whom you crucified . . . Re-
pent, and be baptized every one of you in the name of Jesus Christ
for the forgiveness of your sins." (Acts 2:36, 38b)

This account in Acts, the Great Commission in Matthew 28:19,
20; Jesus' reference to his own work in Mark 1:38; and other

passages tell Christians today what the first followers of Jesus knew God had commissioned them to do. They were chosen to witness, and there has been no change in this charge since New Testament times.

Those who are followers of Jesus Christ and members of his fellowship are God's people, related to him by the New Covenant made by Jesus Christ. The church is God's church, created by his activity in human history. The task of all who are members of God's church is to share with others their own experience of God's forgiving love revealed in the life, death, and resurrection of Jesus Christ.

These are familiar statements, so familiar that their meaning may be missed. One reason for the emphasis on mission today is that the church of the twentieth century has sometimes seemed to ignore or forget what is required of it if it is to be the church. When it is tempted to think first of its own comfort, its own program, its resources and size, the church is in danger of losing its God-given identity. God's first charge to his church is to *witness,* to make his Son known to the ends of the earth. No task is more important than this, and no Christian is exempt from the demands of this charge.

MISSION IN ITS HISTORICAL CONTEXT

In the history of the church this witnessing has taken many forms. The mission has been carried out in many ways. Throughout the New Testament we read accounts of the verbal witnessing of the early followers of Jesus Christ. But there is also evidence of other activities through which Christians made an impact on persons outside the fellowship. The worship of the early Christians, the nature of their common life, their response to physical need, their courage under fire, all these testified to what God meant to his people, the difference the lordship of Jesus Christ made in their lives.

Very early in its history, the church discovered that obedience to God required a stand against some of the social practices and beliefs of the times. Harsh treatment of slaves, infanticide, the degradation of women, the abuse of children were condemned. Followers of Jesus found themselves pleading the cause of the slave, caring for abandoned children, ministering to the sick, raising the status of women in society. Acting as God's representatives led to many kinds of service, but the motivation was always the same, to tell people of God's outpouring, saving love revealed in Jesus Christ, a love that extended to all God's human beings, a love that was urgently seeking to win his children back from their rebellion and disobedience to him.

There have been periods in the history of the church when this sense of mission grew dim or assumed strange and even cruel forms. There have been church leaders who were concerned more with their own status and position than with serving God. Sometimes the truth of the gospel has been threatened by pagan ideas and heresies. But always, when God's community seemed to forget that it belonged to God and not to men, that its only reason for existence was God's work, persons appeared who called the church back to its real nature and purpose. There has been more than one period of reformation and recovery for the church in the past two thousand years.

In our own time, the church is faced with several temptations to stray from its God-given task. As is illustrated by the incident at the beginning of this chapter, there is the temptation to let the professional worker be its only representative to the non-church community and to be interested in persons because of what they have to offer rather than because of their own God-given significance. The church is tempted to forget that it lives not to nurture its own life but rather to give its life in service. It is tempted to think of itself as a human club rather than as a divine fellowship for which God alone determines the entrance requirements. The church is tempted to forget persons who are hard to reach, with whom church people find it hard to communicate, who are "not our kind." The church is tempted to think of some groups in its fellowship as less mature than others, as mission churches in need of supervision by the "older, well-established churches."

But these temptations are being identified for what they are, and the church is trying to recover its true missionary zeal and imperative. The new understanding of mission in the life of the church today, and the great interest this has for church people are evidence of this.

MISSION TODAY

There are other evidences. Several decades ago, a great distinction was made between missionaries and those who supported missionaries. The missionary was the professional who "was sent" by Christians who remained at home. Today there is still an urgent need for the professional missionary, but he is now one among very many dedicated to the mission of the church. An illustration of this is the effort to help all Christians from North America living abroad to think of themselves as representatives of Christ to the non-Christian peoples with whom they come in contact.

Another illustration is the awareness that any decision or activity in life may open a mission frontier. The minister who leaves a comfortable suburban pastorate to serve in an underprivileged area is responding to mission. So is the mother in a housing project who gives an afternoon a week to a Christian education program for non-churched children. So is the layman who tries hard to find a home for a "different" family in a community that has not previously welcomed such a family, and does this because he feels God requires it of him.

In his book, *Our Mission Today,* Tracey Jones points out: "The New Testament speaks of a diversity of gifts but only one missionary responsibility, which is on every member. Furthermore, if contemporary history is teaching us any lesson, it is this:

"The challenges confronting the churches are so massive, so complex, so critical that anything less than the response of the whole membership will not be adequate to meet them. Every Christian must see himself or herself as a missionary of Jesus Christ confronting people in the no man's land between faith and unbelief."[1]

[1] Tracey Jones, *Our Misson Today.* New York, World Outlook Press, 1963, page 126.

Another evidence is the growing awareness on the part of Christian people that all lands are mission lands, that geographical location has nothing to do with older or younger churches, with the quality of spiritual maturity church people possess. It is significant that today over two hundred Asian missionaries have left their own churches to serve in other lands and that some of these have come to the United States where their witness has brought new vitality and spiritual depth to Western Christians. It is significant, too, that many Christian workers from the West are dropping the term "missionary" and identifying themselves as fraternal workers or simply Christian workers in the countries and situations in which they serve.

Still another evidence is the outreach of the church to persons and groups who have been neglected and forgotten. Several years ago, a Protestant social worker employed by a church agency made the charge that most of the young people she knew would never "make it" in the church. Church leaders would not know how to help or even to talk with the delinquent, the young dope addict, the emotional wrecks that were her responsibility, her "congregation." The charge is still tragically true, but it is not as true as it was when it was made. Committed laymen and ministers have sought ways to contact delinquents and addicts, to minister to them, to witness to them that God cares about their misery, their anger, their loneliness, their hurt. Families have moved into urban housing projects to witness by their presence to God's love. With similar zeal and love, churchmen have also sought to reach the handicapped, the institutionalized, and—groups that are often even more difficult to contact—those who have so much material security that they feel no need for the faith of the church.

Teachers of the church participate in this mission as they work with boys and girls and as they work with the families of boys and girls. Teachers are sent into the church school classroom, into the community, into the homes to speak, live, and serve, offering themselves and using their teaching skill in order that every child may respond to God, trust and love him, and want to be one of God's people.

NO BOUNDARIES TO THE MISSION FRONTIER

Today many ways have opened up for carrying on the mission of the church. Many people are given particular responsibilities as missionaries, as workers in specific jobs at home and overseas. But no Christian exists who is not a missionary in the true meaning of the word. His parish may be his own occupational or professional group, the neighborhood in which he lives, the friends with whom he enjoys recreational activities. His method may be the example of his own living, the way he uses his time and money. It may be his spoken word. But the motivation for his witness is always the same: to share with others his experience of what God has done in Jesus Christ in the hope that through the one who witnesses God may speak and become known to those who have not experienced the wonder of his love.

This is what is meant when the word "mission" is used. This is why the church is often described as mission. The basis for this mission is in the New Testament, the recorded works and acts of Jesus Christ and the directive he gave the church, the records left by Paul and other early church leaders. Those who are the fellowship of the church are committed to fulfilling this mission as their primary task and desire.

2: Christian Education, Missionary Education, and Mission Education

What is the relationship between Christian education, missionary education, and mission education? Does each have its own content area, its own unique purpose? Is it theologically and educationally valid to say that missionary education and mission education really belong under the umbrella of Christian education?

Thoughtful leaders of children have asked these questions. They want to be clear in their own minds, and they are puzzled when they find church organizations, agencies, and publications expressing views that seem to conflict with one another or that fail to make any distinctions.

The fact that in past years the church has recognized a difference between missionary education and Christian education is indicated by the organizational structure in many local churches, a structure that has been followed denominationally and interdenominationally. There have been, and still are, a number of separate agencies and interboard committees charged with planning and carrying out specific programs labeled "Christian education" and "missionary education."

The fact that the church has also recognized common purposes and interests is indicated by provisions for cross-representation on the committees responsible for each, cooperation on projects and in the preparation of resource materials, and in some situations, joint committees responsible for Christian and missionary education in the local church. In fact, it is quite common to find that plans for missionary education of children are made by the church agency responsible for Christian education.

Yet the relationships remain ambiguous and continue to be the subject of earnest discussion. Out of these discussions has come an appreciation of the thin and shadowy line that separates missionary education and Christian education, a line that at times seems to disappear, and at others becomes very sharp and divisive.

In these discussions a new phrase has been used, a phrase which has grown in meaning as persons have thought deeply about the nature of the church's educational ministry. This is *mission education*. Mission education refers to more than a study of what the church is doing in its missionary outreach, for central to the concern of mission education is helping persons understand the motivation and nature of their own commitment, their sense of *sentness* or mission in and to the world.

In order to grasp more clearly the relationship between missionary education and Christian education, let us look briefly at the purpose and role each plays in the total educational ministry of the church and then at their kinship with the less familiar concept of mission education.

There are many ideas of what Christian education is and many ways in which churches are organized to carry out Christian education programs. However, Christian education is generally understood to include what a church fellowship does to help its people come to know God as he is revealed in Jesus Christ, and to respond to God in faith, trust, and self-giving. Implied in this understanding is an awareness that a person's relationship to God deepens and matures through his continuing experience in the church fellowship, and that God depends upon persons to help one another grow in their Christian life and faith.

To achieve this purpose, churches produce materials that help teachers guide learners in understanding and living the biblical faith. Churches have age-group organizations so that individuals may be taught and encouraged to learn under conditions appropriate to their needs and capacities. Churches have leadership training programs to enable those who work with children, youth, and adults to understand the faith they seek to communicate to the age-group they will teach, the nature of the environment in which learning is encouraged, and the methods that stimulate growth. And churches have developed many types of educational activities in addition to the Sunday church school, such as vacation church schools, camps, weekday programs, and family programs, to involve persons in Christian nurture.

One of the major Christian education activities in recent years has been that of curriculum development. Christian educators have tried to bring together the best insights from general education, human development, and other fields, and to use these in strengthening the curriculum of the church. Some of this work has been done by denominational, some by interdenominational groups. Two outcomes of this study are particularly significant for those interested in the relationship of Christian and missionary education.

The first is a new understanding of the nature of curriculum itself. Curriculum is far more than specific materials or programs. Curriculum, rightly understood, is *all that is planned* to help persons grow toward the purpose of Christian education, however a church states this purpose. Curriculum includes the physical environment, the teacher, the lesson material, the planned activities, the teacher-student relationships, the relationships students have with one another, and that hard-to-define but important element, the spirit or atmosphere in which the educational program takes place.

A second significant outcome of the work is an analysis of the key elements in curriculum. One element is *purpose*. Because curriculum is the organized plan of the church to carry on its ministry of Christian education, the purpose of curriculum must be identical with the purpose of Christian education.

A second element is the *setting* in which Christian education occurs, or the "context" of curriculum as this is frequently stated.

This is, and can only be, the fellowship of the Christian community wherever this fellowship is present: in a church building on Sunday morning, in a summer camp, in a Christian family.

The third element has been identified as *scope and content*. The scope includes every area of learning that will encourage growth in relationship to God. Recognizing the impossibility of projecting the potential scope in any systematic program, it then becomes necessary to identify—and to separate from the possible scope—the essential and basic areas of Christian education which can be taught and learned. These basic areas then become the content of a curriculum program.

Teachers of children are familiar with many content areas included in the curriculum of the children's division—the life of Jesus Christ, Old Testament leaders, the nature of the church, the world God created, worship, Christian living, the ministry of Paul, the missionary outreach of the church. Teachers of children are also aware of how much might be included but is not. God is the Lord of every area of life, and every area of life is rightfully the subject of Christian interpretation in the church. But the situation in which Christian education occurs necessitates limiting this potential scope to the actual content that can be offered. The age and capacities of children also dictate what wisely can be included in content for a specific group or class.

A fourth element in curriculum is teaching-learning *methodology*. How does a teacher communicate the Christian gospel so that it may be understood, so that its meaning will become part of the life of the learner? How does the five-year-old learn about Jesus Christ? How does the second-grader learn to know and to respond to God? How is the sixth-grader guided in his understanding of the gospel's significance for all his relationships? How do persons of various ages learn? What happens when learning really takes place? What conditions need to be present? Answers to these questions indicate teaching-learning methods that may be used in the Christian education program.

Finally, effective curriculum has an *organizing principle* that relates purpose, context or setting, content, scope, and method. This organizing principle may be the orderly study of the Bible, the principle that guides the uniform lesson program, which has had a place in the church for almost a century. Or the principle may be the church year, a central theme of the Christian faith, or a more educationally focused principle such as a plan for helping persons encounter the gospel as they grow up in the Christian community.

Along with its study of curriculum, Christian education has been concerned with the development of leadership, grading and grouping of children in the church, the nature of Christian learning, insights from the field of human development, and especially with understanding the biblical and theological foundations of its work. One important result of the great theological interest of Christian education has been a renewed sense of the central place of the Holy Spirit in the teaching-learning process. The teacher does not see himself in control of the educational program. He is an agent of God, a channel through which the Holy Spirit may work. The Holy Spirit is the educator in the worshiping, witnessing, and working fellowship.

Christian education, then, is an important ministry of the church. It is concerned with helping persons meet God and grow in their faith and response to him as he has revealed himself in Jesus Christ. Christian education is organized for work with its staff of teachers and officers, its committee or board or commission, its program, its curriculum. If this is the purpose and nature of Christian education, what then have we meant by *missionary education*? What has been its distinctive responsibility?

Missionary education, as it was carried on in the recent past, had its own program materials, its own distinctive organization and groups, its own leadership and administration. In missionary education, persons learned about areas of the world in which missionaries were at work, the needs of non-Christian people for the good news of the gospel, denominational missionary activities, and leaders who were sent to make the gospel known. "Foreign" and "home" missions were distinguished by the geographical relationship of the area covered to the group planning the study or by the denominational board which had the responsibility for supervising the area.

Frequently missionary education was carried on in special programs, and children were invited to join mission-study groups. A number of churches had a monthly "Mission Sunday."

The purpose of missionary education included helping persons become familiar with denominational missions, developing an interest in what was being done, increasing support for this work, and encouraging children and young people to consider missionary service as their life vocation.

In a number of churches what has been described here still has a very important part in the life of the church. What then has happened to change the terminology from missionary education to *mission education?*

The answer is a growing conviction that the biblical concept of mission eliminates any theological distinction between home and foreign missions, between the missionary and other Christians. Every Christian is involved in mission. Every Christian in the truest sense of the word is a "missionary" to his neighbor outside the church, whether this neighbor lives next door or halfway around the world. Because of this, the concept of *mission education* has gained the respect and loyalty of persons committed to both Christian education and missionary education.

Mission education is concerned with helping all Christians develop the understandings, skills, and attitudes that will make them effective representatives of Christ in mission—his people, continuing his work.

There is a difference between this and simply supporting missions or another's missionary activity. The person who knows himself to be Christ's representative will still support missions in areas where he cannot witness directly, but he will also be Christ's emissary in every event of his daily life. His witness may be verbal. It will be revealed in attitude and behavior. For Christ's representative, the mission field is his home, neighborhood, and world. His mission field is not confined to areas in which organized programs of mission work are in existence.

Today mission education in the local church is concerned about changing attitudes, increasing knowledge, and stimulating participation in home and world missionary enterprises. It is concerned with helping persons know themselves as missionaries, engaged in continuing the mission of Jesus Christ. Because of this, it is also committed to helping persons make known the saving love of God to all—next door and around the world—who have not heard the good news of the Christian gospel.

To make it possible to work toward the achievement of this purpose, responsibility for mission education usually is lodged in a group of persons in the local church who will see that activities, resources, and leadership are available for the mission education program. In some denominations, this may be the same committee, commission, or board chosen to act for the church in the area of Christian education.

In the children's division, mission education is usually included in the ongoing program of Christian education. Certain units in the Sunday church school and weekday curriculum will naturally highlight it more specifically than others. In addition, special programs, such as family nights, Sunday evening meetings, and Schools of Missions, often include children in mission study sessions. Vacation Church Schools and additional sessions also provide opportunities for mission education.

The committee responsible for mission education seeks the best possible leaders and helps them train for their task. Often these leaders are regular church school teachers. They may be persons with a special interest and background in mission education. They may be people who have been active in a home or world mission enterprise. Always they need to be persons with a deep and growing commitment to mission.

The committee helps to see that these leaders have the resources they require to do effective work. This includes mission study units planned by denominations for age-group use and units prepared by denominations working together. In the unit materials there is usually a listing of recommended supplementary resources. Over a period of time the committee responsible for mission education should gradually build up a library of supplementary resources for the teachers' use.

Persons who review mission study units prepared for use in the children's division of the church will find a wide range of subject matter. The scope of mission education rightfully includes 1) all areas of human life in which witness is needed; 2) the biblical imperative to mission; 3) the need of men to know God; and 4) the responsibility of his people to be his emissaries to others and to one another.

From this potential scope, themes are selected for study. The choice of these themes is influenced by important mission frontiers, new developments in mission activity and awareness, and the age groups with which the themes will be used. For example, both a general theme, such as "Affluence and Poverty: Dilemma for Christians," and a geographical theme, such as "The Christian Mission on the Rim of East Asia," have been chosen by denominations in the National Council of Churches' Department of Education for Mission (Friendship Press).

During the boys' and girls' years in the children's division of the church, the content of mission education includes opportunities to learn about:

• Great leaders of the church, past and present, who have demonstrated in their lives and work at home and abroad what it means to be a missionary.

• "Ordinary people," including boys and girls, who have been missionaries in routine as well as in dramatic situations.

• The child's own involvement in mission in the situations in which he lives—his church, family, school, and playground.

• The mission story of the church beginning with the events recorded in Acts and continuing to the present day.

• The mission enterprises of the child's own denomination, what is being done, what more needs to be done, how children can witness in the situations in which they live.

• The mission enterprise of the ecumenical fellowship—what churches need to do and are doing together.

• What is happening in the world today that affects the mission outreach of the church, the failures and successes of the church, areas of crisis and unusual need.

• The worldwide nature of the Christian fellowship, which unites men of many different races, nations, languages, and political loyalties.

• Where some of the most urgent needs for mission activity are, including those "next door," in the child's own neighborhood, and the opportunities the child has for witness and mission service.

• The motivations and skills that are part of a commitment to mission: the abilities children need to develop if their witness is to be effective, why the Christian has to share the meaning God's love and care have for him, how children can share their enthusiasm for their church with others.

• The resources of the Christian fellowship, which strengthen those who face ridicule, loneliness, even danger while witnessing for God. These resources include the supporting strength of the fellowship itself, which is of vital importance to children; the knowledge that the person witnessing today is a member of a long line of courageous persons who have made obedience to God primary in their lives; and the power available from God in Christ who has promised to be with all who "go and make disciples of all nations."

How this content comes into the programs planned for boys and girls will be dealt with more specifically in Chapter 3.

From this discussion of Christian education and mission education in the life of the church, it is clear that the lines between the two cannot be sharply drawn. There is overlapping in content —neither dares lay exclusive claim to the ministry and message of Paul; in program—mission education belongs in the Sunday church school as much as Christian education; even in purpose— effective witness cannot be made without a deepening personal relationship to God.

Yet, because of church organization, because of the interests of children's leaders, and because a significant difference in focus does exist, a distinction is possible.

Christian education is committed to helping persons become aware of God as he is revealed in Jesus Christ, to respond in faith, trust, and self-giving, and to mature in their understanding of what the Christian faith is and in their ability to live as Christians in all areas of their lives.

Mission education is committed to *helping persons who know God* to grow in their desire to witness to others of what God has done for them, in their ability to be God's representatives, and in their understanding of where witness is urgently needed. Mission education includes education about missions, about great missionary leaders, about denominational mission programs, as well as developing skills in witnessing, learning the critical frontiers in which witness is urgently needed, and deepening the motivation to witness.

There are some who will continue to use the term *missionary education* rather than *mission education*. Missionary education is a good term, but for many it will continue to refer primarily to a very significant content area in mission education—the study of missions, the biblical basis for mission, the missionary enterprise, and great mission leaders. Mission education will be used in this book to include all of these, as well as *learning to fulfill our God-given responsibility to witness*.

This understanding of mission education does not introduce a new concept into the God-given function of the church. But for teachers of children, mission education holds some intriguing possibilities that deserve to be more fully explored. For example, what are the crucial mission areas in the life of the church in which children can effectively witness? What opportunities are present in the school and neighborhood? What is reasonable to expect of children in the secular society in which much of their lives is lived?

How can children be prepared for their witness? How can their basic needs be met so they have the strength and capacity to witness? What attitudes and skills do children need to develop if they are to witness effectively and naturally?

What support must the adult fellowship be ready to give boys and girls who take seriously their roles as God's representatives?

How seriously does the adult fellowship take the implications of mission education as far as boys and girls are concerned? How can the local church exemplify and communicate to children the spirit of mission?

How, therefore, can all of those engaged in the church's ministry to children unite in helping them to grow up in the mission of the church?

These are important questions, which deserve answers if the church is to help its boys and girls understand and respond to the missionary spirit of the church in the world in which children live.

3: Children and Mission Education

Children growing up in the latter part of the twentieth century sometimes seem to be a new kind of humanity! Parents who once confidently helped boys and girls with their schoolwork admit that they are intellectually outdistanced by their fifth- and sixth-graders. Social maturity and the intriguing, perplexing problems of adolescence seem to be catching up with youngsters earlier than they did a generation ago. Teachers of boys and girls in the church are amazed by the questions that are raised, the amount of information and misinformation children possess, the response and lack of response to church programs and activities.

It is clear that in some very real ways today's children do differ from the youngsters of a generation or two ago. Yet in many very significant ways they do not. What do we know about boys and girls, how they learn and grow, the influences that are affecting their interests and purposes in life? And what does this knowledge say to church leaders concerned about educating these boys and girls for mission?

Let us look first at the children themselves, then at the nature of learning, and finally at some characteristics of the world that is the learning environment of today's children.

THE CHILD

Children are persons endowed with the miraculous characteristics granted by God to all men—they are not putty to be shaped into adult-desired forms. Nor are they miniature adults.

One of the child's most exciting characteristics is his tremendous capacity for growth. Every living human being is born with this God-given potentiality, which is both orderly and extremely complex.

During the period of childhood, physical, social, emotional, and intellectual growth take place at a very rapid rate if boys and girls receive the kinds of help they need to make this growth possible. If this help is not received, growth is stunted, and stunting in one area of growth inevitably affects other areas.

Those who work with children in the church are aware of a tremendous potentiality for spiritual development. But this, too, may be dwarfed if it is not fed and nurtured. Children are particularly dependent upon people for the kinds of nourishment on which their spiritual development relies. It is almost as though God were saying to parents and teachers and all adults who are related to boys and girls, "I am counting on you to help these boys and girls know me, trust me, and serve me. I have made no other plans except to work through you." God works through people and trusts them to communicate the gospel of his love to each new generation.

Sensitive adults who accept this responsibility are aware of an orderly process in spiritual growth just as they are aware of a developmental process in social and physical maturation. The capacity for religious understanding and response possessed by a child of two is quite different from that possessed by children who are four or eight or ten. It does no good to try to hurry the process nor to coerce children into a response for which they are not yet ready. The preschool child must not be expected to have the understanding of God nor the relationship with him that is possible for a sixth-grader. Nor does a preschool child witness to the meaning church has for him in the manner of his more grown-up brother and sister.

There is danger in trying to hurry growth. There is also danger in retarding the process, in not providing children with the resources and stimuli they need for achieving their potential. Church leaders need to be on the alert against this, as well as against the temptation to expect from youngsters more than they are ready to give.

Every child can grow. Every child grows in his own way. The uniqueness of individual human growth is another God-given characteristic of persons. Each child is a distinctive self. His appearance and personality are unduplicated. He is an unrepeatable event in the history of the world. This means that every attempt to describe the "average child" for a particular age must be recognized as a flexible generalization, for in reality there can be no "average child."

This unduplicated nature of each child influences learning expectations in two important ways: how much each child will learn and what each child will learn. No two children have identical capacities, skills, and abilities.

If you are a teacher, think of the boys and girls with whom you work. Recall what you know about the abilities, interests, and needs of each boy and girl in your group. Ponder the kinds of responses to the events and activities of your program. What sets each child apart from the others? What unique capacities has each one revealed to you? Children share common interests, it is true, but they never respond in exactly the same manner to a given situation.

Because of this, teachers must be ready to give individual support and help at the points where it is needed and not expect every child to grow at the same rate in the same ways. God did not create people to be alike. Teachers neither can nor should attempt to reverse God's plan.

Another quality of persons is the fact that everyone must do his own learning. No teacher or parent can learn for a child, and the fact that a teacher knows something and communicates this to children, does not mean that the children have grasped what the teacher has in mind. Each child picks and chooses from what is offered to him, retaining what has meaning and significance for him. Even facts that are given back to a teacher in the form in which they have been taught may have a very different meaning for children from the meaning the teacher intends.

Teachers who assume that the simple communication of religious content guarantees that this content will become important in the lives of boys and girls, are treading on precarious ground. Each child created by God is endowed with capacities, needs, interests uniquely his own. These influence what each child learns, and make learning an individual matter.

THE ENVIRONMENT IN WHICH LEARNING OCCURS

In Old Testament times the family and the tribe provided the teaching-learning environment for children. Fathers passed on to their boys and girls the great convictions and stories of their people. Mothers and fathers witnessed in the family to what their faith meant to them. Holy day celebrations, the weekly Sabbath observances, family practices all were taught. Children grew up in a God-oriented environment.

Today's Complex Culture. The contrast of Old Testament times with today is striking. Children are exposed to many conflicting influences and pressures in this late twentieth-century world. They are not living in a religious society. Science has its devotees. Status and money are important goals. Men and women declare sadly but earnestly, "We can't be financial successes in business today and practice the Christian ethic."

Children are aware of the importance attached to science, to money, to social position. The are also aware of other perplexing events and pressures in their world. Many youngsters have no real family life. They live in one-parent homes or are raised by relatives. Tens of thousands move frequently and have to learn how to adjust quickly to new schools, new neighborhoods, new friends. They have no chance to put down roots in a real home community. There is increasing pressure to "make good" academically, a pressure which is particularly difficult for some boys and girls to handle.

The environment of children today is a confused, complex affair. It is far different from the religiously oriented society of the Old Testament times.

There is another factor in the child's world which church leaders cannot ignore. This is the presence and influence of the adult world. Events which boys and girls are neither emotionally nor intellectually ready to understand come to them in dramatic form through mass communication media. Violence, unscrupulous behavior, a false concept of what is really desirable are brought to children's attention through stories, pictures, and advertising.

Children are also sensitive to the general anxiety shared by adults facing the possibility and implications of nuclear, chemical, and biological warfare. Children wonder about evident injustices in society and "why somebody doesn't do something about them." The adult world often makes very little sense to boys and girls, yet it is increasingly their world, and they have to deal with it. They may be fortunate in finding wise adult friends who will help them think through the problems and questions they have. But often youngsters are left to struggle alone with some overwhelming issues.

Children who come into groups planned by the church bring with them all that has happened to them in the world outside the church. They bring the meaning of their family life or lack of it, the events that have occurred in the school classroom, world news and the way persons important to children have reacted to it, and their experiences in neighborhood play groups.

Children also bring themselves, the native capacities and potentialities God has given them, their family heritage, and their feeling about themselves and others which has grown out of all their experiences. When teachers look at the boys and girls who face them in a particular class or group, teachers see amazingly complex, wonderful persons.

The Many Teachers of Children. There was a time when public school leaders told parents to follow a "hands off" policy in the intellectual training of their children. There was a time when church leaders said the same thing about religious training. Today both school and church know that education is not so easily controlled. Church leaders are keenly aware that much of what boys and girls learn and believe about the Christian faith will be gained outside the regular curriculum of the church, for there are many teachers of children who influence their learning and growth.

Parents are teachers. Children are deeply affected by what parents are, do, and believe. Parents who are active in the church because they are earnest, enthusiastic followers of Jesus Christ communicate their loyalty to their boys and girls. Parents who attend church out of a sense of duty or because it is "the thing to do" witness to the very different meaning the church holds in their lives.

Every person in contact with a child is a potential teacher. Adult conversation, what members of the child's peer group do and think, the attitudes of neighbors, the relationship church-related men and women have with a child, what popular and unpopular school teachers do and say—all these influences have educational significance for boys and girls. Children bring the meanings they have garnered in these contacts to the sessions planned by church leaders. These meanings may stand in the way of what a teacher hopes a child will learn, or they may give wings to what happens in the church program. It is important for teachers to be sensitive to the meanings children acquire from the different teachers who populate a child's world.

THE LEARNING PROCESS

Up to this point certain statements have been made about children and the influences that affect their learning and growth:

• Children are persons with a God-given capacity for growth that depends upon help from others if growth is to take place.

• Every child has his own unique style of growth.

• Every child must do his own learning.

• Children today live in a complex culture that exposes them to many perplexing problems and ideas, and these problems and ideas influence what they learn and are able to learn in the fellowship of the church.

• Children have many teachers, and some are neither responsible to nor motivated by the faith of the church.

In the light of the situation these statements reveal, how do children learn? What factors determine when learning is possible? More specifically, what conditions must teachers seek if the church fellowship is to educate its children successfully in the mission of the church?

As part of their study of the church in Africa, Ellen's class worked on a model African village. The purpose of the project was to stimulate the interest of the class in the Christian people of Africa and the influence Christians have in the lives of others.

The members of the class were intrigued with the African homes, and each child wanted to build his own. But the teacher of the class was very eager to have the village completed so it could be displayed at a parents' open house. She felt the work would go faster if some children finished the houses while others worked on other details of the village.

The children rebelled. "You don't learn about African homes unless you make one," Ellen declared. "We really aren't doing this to learn about the houses," the teacher answered. "We're learning about the church in Africa." "Well, I like the house," Ellen responded. "I want to finish mine, and no one else can touch it." The other children supported Ellen. The teacher reluctantly gave in with the reminder that parents would be disappointed if the class had no work on display. The children did not seem to care.

What was happening in this situation? What were the children really learning?

An adult who observed and reported the incident suggested that these children were probably not gaining much insight into the meaning of the Christian faith in the lives of African people. They were learning something about the houses in a particular section of Africa. They were also learning a questionable motivation for class plans and activities: to have something to "show."

What went wrong? In order to understand this, it is necessary to have in mind some of the essential facts about the learning process.

One: persons learn when they feel a need to learn or have an interest in learning. The boy with the new bike works hard to master the mechanics of riding. The child who senses the power granted by the ability to read will concentrate for a surprisingly long period on acquiring this skill. Boys practice catching and batting to make the team. The toddler is up and down, up and down as he struggles to learn to walk. When a person wants to know something badly enough, he will make a great effort to learn it. Motivation is essential to learning.

Two: persons learn when they have access to resources that make learning possible. These resources may be the physical capacity of the child and the encouragement of adults who stimulate the toddler to stand upright and take the first steps. The resources may be the coaching of an understanding father who helps with batting practice. They may be the school environment, appropriate books, and a trained teacher for the child learning to read. All learning needs help from the human and physical environment and depends upon its being available.

Three: persons learn when they have the time to learn. Some knowledge and skills are quickly acquired. Some demand a lifetime. Genuine learning is possible only when there is the needed time to think, to study, to reflect, and, if a skill is involved, to practice. One of the frequent criticisms of Christian education is the limited time available for the teaching program of the church and the quantity of content learning that is sometimes crowded into this time. People are not allowed to live with the great ideas and meanings of the Christian faith. Children are rushed through study themes in the Sunday church school. Learning is jeopardized when it is hurried.

Four: people learn when they find some use for the insight, knowledge, or skill they have acquired. It is easy to see how the toddler uses his new walking skill, how the teenager makes use of his ability to drive a car. Often it is not so easy to discover how a new idea or a changed attitude is put to work. But if they have become a part of a person, they will be.

A young woman on a world trip found herself temporarily stranded in a small village in Asia. She became acquainted with some of the people of the village and learned why they followed the customs of dress and food she at first thought bizarre. When she returned to her own community, she remarked that this experience was one of the most valuable she ever had. "Never again will I think that just because I do something a certain way it is the only way to do it. What is right for me may be very wrong for many others." This is an illustration of genuine learning.

Reviewing the experience of Ellen's class with these principles in mind, it is not hard to see at least a few of the mistakes that were made. The children had developed no real interest in the Christian people of Africa. They had no reason for being interested. If they had resources for helping them find out about the African church, they were not stimulated to use these resources. They were pressed for time, and the real goal of the project was a parents' exhibit, not a new relationship to the African church, its influence, and its work.

One important question needs to be raised: the preceding paragraphs describe the process by which we learn skills and knowledge and attitudes; but is this the way faith comes and the way persons are motivated to share the wonder of their faith with others?

There is no clear answer. How faith emerges in human life is a mystery. Yet Christian teachers may be confident God has committed to them the responsibility to "make disciples," to carry on the work he started through his son, Jesus Christ; and that God depends upon them to use the skill and wisdom they possess to make their teaching effective. Teachers may also be sure that if they do the best they can in the situations in which they are called to teach, they can safely leave what they cannot do and what is not theirs to do in the hands of God.

COMPONENTS OF MISSION EDUCATION

In the light of what is known about the conditions for learning and the God-given potential children have to learn and grow, how do teachers help boys and girls understand and want to participate in the mission of the church? What must be provided for children if the nature of mission is to take on real meaning for them?

A Personal Experience of the Church. Every child needs a personal experience of the church fellowship, of its loving concern for and interest in him, before he can want to invite others to share in his church. This experience may come to children in a number of ways: through a significant relationship with some adults who represent the church fellowship to a boy or girl; through a realization that he and his family, although active in different areas of the church's life, are part of the same Christian fellowship; and through his Sunday church school class. For older boys and girls, the meaning of the church fellowship will be richer and more complete than it will be for younger children. But for every child the meaning must be more than verbal. Children are convinced of the importance of the church and of its redemptive love only when the words used by teachers are verified in the child's personal life.

One Sunday morning, just before church school time, Bruce learned that his family would be moving again at the close of the school year. The thought of leaving his friends upset Bruce, and he was in an angry mood when he entered his fifth-grade class. The teacher sensed that something was wrong when Bruce jostled several children and pushed some hymn books from a chair.

Quietly the teacher took Bruce aside and remarked that something must be troubling him. The boy was startled. He had expected a scolding for what he knew was inappropriate behavior. Instead he found understanding and sympathy. The story of the move was reported. "We'll miss you, Bruce," the teacher said. "I'm sorry you are leaving us. Will you send us your new address? I'd like to let the church in your new home town know how much you have helped our class."

Bruce relaxed and joined the other children. At the close of the session, he told the teacher, "I'll be sure to send that address."

At an important crisis in his life, a crisis that could have influenced his feeling about his parents, his friends, his church, and himself, Bruce's church through its representative, his teacher, gave him the kind of help and support he needed. Bruce experienced the meaning of the caring, loving fellowship.

Worship. If children are to share in the mission of the church, they need to find the strength and wisdom for witness that can come only through worship.

When they worship, children recognize their dependence upon God, their need for him. Their awareness of God's concern for all members of his human family is deepened. They receive guidance in how God wants them to serve. They can ask for and receive forgiveness for times when they have failed to act as God's children. They can rejoice and praise God for his abundant gifts. Through worship children share the life of the Christian community, which is a worshiping community.

Children may be deprived of this experience of worship when a planned service, a routine, is substituted for the real event. Worship may and often does occur in such a service, but the service itself is not necessarily worship.

Worship is a personal meeting with God. By definition God must be real to the worshiper. Worship may take place in unexpected moments of awareness when children sense the presence of God. Worship may happen as boys and girls join in a carefully prepared program of praise and prayer and thanksgiving. However it occurs, children need access to God's strength and wisdom through genuine worship, and children need to experience the church as a worshiping community.

A Theological Concept of the Church. Children in training for participation in the mission of the church need an intellectual as well as experiential understanding of what the church is. As the child learns how the church began, what activities and concerns occupied the earliest members of the church, what the church meant to people living in New Testament times and in various periods in its history, his awareness of the church is deepened. He begins to formulate his own theological statement of the nature of the church.

In addition to this introductory acquaintance with the meaning of the church as God's fellowship of people who are obedient to him, children need to learn something about the distinctive nature of their own denominational group. They need to meet the men and women who have been denominational leaders, learn what they stood and worked for, what they stood against and why, and what they contributed to the church's mission. Through imaginatively entering into the experiences of these persons, boys and girls are able to enlarge their understanding of what "the Christian church" really signifies and stands for.

Knowledge of How the Church Has Fulfilled Its Mission. Children need some acquaintance with the ways in which the church has fulfilled its mission, how it has acted and served in different times and places. This includes not only knowledge of the great dramatic periods in the life of the church and the men and women who become famous for their missionary activity, but also the less exciting but quietly effective events in which the church has worked for God.

The events themselves are important, but even more important is the motivation for mission. Older children can begin to see that service to others is not necessarily motivated by the urgent desire to share with others the good news that God is a loving God and cares for all his children. There are many reasons for service. Persons may serve for an expected reward, because the consequence of failing to act is more painful than the effort involved in serving, or because of friendship and concern.

Service activities stimulated by the conviction that "This is how I can make known to others what God's love means to me" are rooted in a sense of mission. This is the motive that has led the missionary leaders of the church, past and present, to risk all that they have in obedience to God's call.

An Understanding of the Church's Weaknesses. Another ingredient of mission education is understanding that the human church has not always been faithful to its mission, that today participation in the mission of the church may be difficult, and that people are weak and often turn aside from the tasks God gives to them. It is unfair to children to imply that church leaders are perfect and completely faithful to God's calling.

When children are old enough to distinguish in their thinking between the human and divine aspects of the life of the church, they can grasp the theological aspects of this problem.

In the meantime, boys and girls know all too well that Christians can be unfriendly, thoughtless, selfish. Christians sometimes do twist the truth. They may fail to give others the respect and dignity God's children deserve.

What children may not realize is that the church exists because people do sin, that persons come into the fellowship of the church because it is a redemptive fellowship in which God's forgiving love is present. Jesus Christ came to save sinners, to heal those who do not do what they know they should, but instead do what they know they should not.

Human sin influences the corporate life of the church, and there have been and still are times when this community of Christ fails to be obedient to God's will. The remarkable thing is that the temptation of the church to disobey God has never gone unchecked. Again and again in its history men and women have risen as Luther did to remind the church what it really is and what is its sole authority.

Children who know that temptation, failure, and sin are not alien to the life of the human church are well prepared for the difficulties they will often meet in their own witness. Some of these difficulties may seem minor to adults, but in the eyes of children they loom large. Accepting the ridicule of older boys and girls because one is related to the church, the teasing of one's peers, standing up for a child when members of the peer group reject him, refusing to be dishonest, voluntarily giving up a prized outing because of a church commitment, all require loyalty, stamina, and courage.

Children who are tempted to disobey what they know is God's will and who yield to this temptation, need to know they are not alone in their weakness. God does forgive and grant a new start. Even the most courageous leaders of the church have experienced the need for forgiveness over and over again. The church is God's fellowship, but it is not a fellowship of saints who are without sin.

A Disciplined Life. Mission education includes training in the skills of witnessing and in disciplined Christian living. Christian witness and Christian living do involve attitudes and behavior that must be learned in the fellowship of the church, and children need help and support in this learning.

The specific skills may be described in many words. They vary with the age of children and the situations in which children live. But certainly these skills include a growing sensitivity to the rights and feelings of other people, as well as attitudes and behavior that respect these rights; a developing capacity to accept responsibility and the stamina to live with one's mistakes and to learn from them; the ability to disagree without being disagreeable, to handle injustice without becoming bitter, to sacrifice personal desire in the interest of the greater good; the experience of worship, of having a sense of God's steadying presence in every event of life.

Children learn these skills when they live with people who believe in them and practice them. Children do not learn them simply by being told that this is the way "God wants you to live." Nor do they learn how to witness just by hearing stories of missionary heroes, helpful as these stories may be. Witnessing is both a product of Christian living and the ability and desire to tell others of one's own experience of God. This is gained through participation in a community of persons who take seriously their life of discipleship and their responsibility to help others grow in the qualities discipleship demands.

Participation in Mission Activities. Mission education includes opportunities to participate in mission activities and to understand what is being done and why. Children learn to serve through serving, by helping whenever they see a need they can meet—by active support of denominational and interdenominational projects, by their prayers for the mission of the church and through their awareness of what their regular church offering is and what it does.

They learn to witness through opportunities to share with others their experience of the church and their own growing faith in God as revealed in Jesus Christ.

Many opportunities for participation in mission are suggested by the local church, by the mission boards of your denomination, and by interdenominational agencies. Some opportunities will come from groups of neighborhood churches which sponsor community projects. Some will arise out of needs observed by leaders of children and the children themselves.

Whatever the project, whatever the need which the children seek to meet, it is essential that they feel that what they do is important to God and important to them. If the value of the activity is clear only to a leader or a mission board, if the children do not respect and believe in what they are doing, they are deprived of experiences that will help them grow in the awareness that they can and must help when God shows them a need.

To some extent all of these aspects of mission education are pertinent in all areas of the children's division of the church. Yet their specific form will be very different in the different departments and age groups. The capacities, backgrounds, needs, and interests of the children account for these differences.

Every child will not make equal use of the educational opportunities offered to him. Every child will not make the same use. Some children will move slowly, held back by questions raised in their homes, by neighborhood and school experiences, by their native capacity and lack of capacity for certain kinds of learning. Some children will respond quickly. Some children may seem to make no headway at all.

Probably few, if any, boys and girls will achieve more than a beginning understanding of any of these areas. Spiritual maturity of behavior and attitudes are lifelong goals. Mission education is a lifelong pilgrimage with ever-deepening insights and commitments and ever-broadening opportunities for service. But it begins in the children's division with youngsters who are welcomed by Jesus into his father's kingdom, who are eager to show others the way, and who respond to the training and guidance in witness that Christian teachers bring to them.

Mission education, then, is an endeavor of the total Christian community. It comes into the lives of boys and girls through the ministry of adult leaders who are aware that the Christian fellowship is in history to witness to God's saving love. These leaders try to help boys and girls to become aware of God's love in their own lives and to acquire the wisdom, knowledge, and skills that make it possible for persons to witness effectively to others.

Education for mission cannot be confined to any one program

or activity of the church. It cannot be said to happen exclusively in any situation. It is going on in the life of the fellowship whenever the fellowship looks outward into the world of people where God's representatives are called to serve and asks how persons become equipped for this service, so that what they do and say is a testimony to what God has done for them.

Yet mission education is not without its content, its discipline, its administration, and organization. Let us look at these and ask ourselves what the local church can plan so that all its boys and girls may have the opportunity to grow up with a will to mission.

PART II

"You shall be my witnesses . . ."

But you shall receive power
when the Holy Spirit has come upon you;
and you shall be my witnesses in
Jerusalem and in all Judea and Samaria
and to the end of the earth.
Acts 1:8

4: The Teacher and Mission Education

Today we hear it said that the Holy Spirit is the teacher in the educational ministry of the church. Credit is also given to the total church fellowship. Following a presentation in a church school leaders' meeting in which these two statements were made, a children's teacher remarked in earnest bewilderment, "If the church fellowship teaches and the Holy Spirit teaches, what do I do?"

The New Testament account of the early Christian community is clear about the work of the Holy Spirit in the lives of those who witnessed for God. In the first chapter of Acts, the disciples of Jesus Christ were told not to leave Jerusalem until the power of the Holy Spirit had come to them. Then they were to serve as God's representatives to the ends of the earth. Teachers today know that faith *is* God's gift, the work of his Holy Spirit in human life. They cannot *teach* others to trust and believe in God.

Christian teachers are also clear about the educational influence of the entire Christian community. Children of the church do not start learning the moment they enter a class, or stop when the class session is over. The spirit and life of the total fellowship communicate to children. All the relationships and experiences children have in the church have educational meaning whether these relationships and experiences happen within the confines of the church building, in Christian homes, or in other situations where Christians gather.

THE TEACHER'S CONTRIBUTIONS

But what does this leave for the class teacher, the leader of a mission study group, and all the adults who have accepted a specific responsibility for the mission education of boys and girls? What do they do? How important is their task? What are the teacher's distinctive contributions?

One: with the exception of his parents and others in his home, a child's teacher is usually the adult he knows best in the church. Because of this, teachers have a significant influence on the child's understanding of what an adult Christian is like. Children respond to what their teachers do, what they believe, their attitudes, their actions.

This does not mean that teachers are required to be perfect. Neither God nor the church expects perfection from those appointed to be the church's representatives to boys and girls. But teachers are called to be faithful and to recognize that the kind of persons they are does count. Teachers who are enthusiastic about their discipleship, who believe in what they are teaching, who have a deep respect for persons including all members of their classes, who are strong enough to admit their mistakes and wise enough not to try to bluff out of them, are the teachers children need. For teachers have influence. Knowing them helps to shape children's understanding of what a Christian man or woman is like.

Two: the teacher of children is a resource person who helps boys and girls become acquainted with the major ideas, events, and persons of their Christian heritage. As a teacher in the mission education program of the church, he makes available to those in his class information about persons who have been God's representatives in the past, what they accomplished, why they believed in the crucial significance of what they did. The teacher offers to children news about the mission activities and frontiers of the church in their own time.

Sometimes teachers do this by speaking of what they know.

Sometimes teachers point out sources to which children may turn for answers to questions they have, where information the teacher does not have may be found—the books, pamphlets, pictures, audiovisuals that will help children to probe deeply into the meaning of what they are studying.

To become such resource persons, those who are teachers need to build their own rich background of information. They need to learn far more than they will communicate to children if they are to respect themselves as teachers and be stimulating guides for the members of their classes. Reading and study contribute to this background, but they are not always the only or the most important sources of information. Alertness to current events; curiosity about community resources; conversations with persons; trips; and an interest in the art, music, games, folk tales of other cultures all help teachers to be informed. And children respond to persons who "know important things," particularly when these persons are able to communicate their knowledge and wisdom in ways that excite and interest boys and girls.

Three: to be a teacher means to be a member of a team. For every child, this team includes not only those who work with him in a particular grade or class but also the persons who have been and will be his teachers in the church. The teaching team has an historical quality that brings together past, present, and future in the educational experience of all boys and girls.

Sometimes the team a child has known is a strong one, and all members have taught well. Sometimes there are weak links in the team. Sometimes there are broken places in the child's relationship to the teaching ministry of the church.

There may be great differences in viewpoints and emphases held important by members of the team. There may be major differences in skills and interests. Yet for every child, the identity of the team and the nature of its influence will be unique.

A young minister who was a part-time associate in a church while he continued work toward his theological degree taught a class of sixth-grade boys and girls engaged in a study of the inner-city church. Some of the children were very sensitive to the problems and needs of persons in the inner city although the minister knew that none of the boys and girls had ever lived in the city. Other class members were indifferent.

At first the minister sought in the homes of the children, for an explanation of the contrasting attitudes, but what he found out did not explain the unusual concern revealed by some boys and girls. He looked further and learned that those who were most concerned had been taught by a woman who was herself deeply involved in meeting the needs of persons in the inner city. The minister knew that his own teaching would be influenced by what this woman had contributed. He was also wise enough to recognize that future teachers of the children would be reckoning with whatever the children learned or failed to learn under his leadership.

No teacher is a lone wolf. Nor does any teacher bear the burden of sole responsibility for what happens to the boys and girls he teaches. Recognizing this, each teacher tries to do his best for his children during the time they are in his care, trusting others to build on and strengthen whatever he has been able to accomplish.

Four: persons as teachers are participants in the mission of the church. They are God's representatives on a very important mission frontier, the mission frontier of a new generation of children.

Adults who grow up in Christian homes and who have never known what it means to be outside the church fellowship may forget that they would not have heard the gospel without the dedicated witness of parents and others.

Just as the professional missionary going to another culture or another land under the orders of his church and chosen vocation learns all he can about the people among whom he will live and work, so the teacher of children takes with equal seriousness his need to know and understand boys and girls. He tries to learn what is important to them, what they are able and ready to study, how they learn, what their big questions are, what influences are shaping their thinking about themselves, others, their world, the Christian faith. He tries to become skillful in the methods and activities that will stimulate the Christian growth of the children he teaches.

He tries to be a real friend to children, to show his genuine love and concern for them. Above all, he asks God to help him recognize, just as the professional missionary does, that the teacher of children may sow and water and cultivate, but it is God that gives the increase. When teachers have done their best, they are willing to entrust the youngsters they know to God, who alone has the right to determine what the outcome will be. After they have taught they can depart, leaving the fulfillment of their work safely in God's hands.

GOD'S CHOSEN SERVANT

To be a teacher is to be a very important person in the life of the church and the life of children. The teacher is an agent of the church and a channel for God's love and grace in the lives of boys and girls. The teacher in the mission education program of the church is the person who puts boys and girls in touch with some of the most significant events, leaders, and tasks in the past and present life of the fellowship. And he hopes fervently that the children he teaches will be active participants in the church's mission. Teachers who are aware of this will neither downgrade the role of the teacher nor underestimate the teacher's influence.

At the same time, teachers will not be overwhelmed by the nature of their task, for God does not ask the impossible of his representatives. He asks simply that they know something of the mission they are asked to communicate and be faithful to their responsibilities.

Teachers do help children know what an adult Christian is. They do share in the teaching ministry of the church and must require of themselves growth in the knowledge and skills this demands. Teachers are members of a team that includes those who work with a particular class in the present and all who have worked and will work with the members of this group in the past and future. And teachers are on a mission, acting as God's representatives to the boys and girls they teach.

For these reasons, teachers honor their work. They know they are not in ultimate control of what happens through their teaching. This is for God to determine. But they are God's chosen persons serving him and their church through their teaching ministry.

5: Planning the Local Church Program

Mission education does not just happen. Back of every program there is planning, and the quality of this planning has a lot to do with what takes place in the lives of children.

Basic to this planning is an organizational structure that makes it possible for people in the church to work together in the development of the program; an awareness of the areas in which decisions about the program are made; an understanding on the part of each teacher of how he works within the organization and program of his church.

THE LOCAL CHURCH ORGANIZATION

Each denomination or larger church fellowship has its own organizational pattern, and one of the tasks of local church leaders is to find out what their church recommends. In many churches the board, committee, or commission on Christian education is responsible for the mission education of children. In some fellowships, the commission, board, or committee on mission education has primary responsibility, but its members work closely with those who oversee the Christian education activities.

The children's work division usually is represented on this committee, board, or commission by a superintendent, teacher, or specially designated leader. This representative communicates to the overall planning group the work, interests, and needs of those who are teaching boys and girls, and in turn, keeps these leaders in the children's division informed about the total church program.

The group responsible for the total church program must make, or delegate the responsibility for making, decisions in a number of important areas, including the following:

• The organization of the age-group program for mission education, the classes or departments in which mission education units will be taught.

• The groups and activities through which the church's program of mission education will be carried out.

• The curriculum of mission education.

• The scheduling of programs and activities.

• The recruitment and training of leaders.

• The evaluation of the church program of mission education.

• The relationship between mission and stewardship education.

Sometimes the general committee, which represents the entire local church fellowship, makes the basic decisions in all these areas. Sometimes it makes general decisions, but delegates more specific decisions to those who will carry them out. For example, a very new church in a very new residential community saw an urgent mission field in its own backyard. The committees on Christian and mission education planned and scheduled a series of Sunday evening meetings on "The Church's Witness in Its Own Neighborhood." Responsibility for working out the age-group programs was entrusted to leaders in the age group divisions.

In another church where there was very little mission zeal, the general committee asked age-group committees to develop an effective program for mission education geared to the interests and capacities of children, youth, and adults. In this situation the decision of the general committee was that there needed to be and should be a program. Experienced age-group leaders determined what, when, and how.

In every church, it is wise and necessary that a representative group of people be responsible for the mission education program. Without such a group, the effectiveness of the mission education program is likely to be spotty and irregular. Ultimately everyone suffers. Boys and girls are particularly vulnerable when there is no such group, because they are completely dependent upon adults for what is planned for them. They have no channels and no power for developing their own program. And they are not likely to want to, since they have not had the experience in the church that lets them know what they are missing.

If you are a teacher with a particular interest in the mission education of children, you may be wondering how this organizational structure is related to your own work, how it may be more effectively related, and the support the organization can provide for mission education in your church.

Let us look at the more important areas in the mission education of children that fall within the responsibility of this general committee and see how age-group leaders and their work are related to the plans and decisions it makes.

AN EFFECTIVE AGE-GROUP ORGANIZATION

Teachers who talk across church lines about class and departmental organization know that there are currently a number of different plans for grouping and grading in the churches. Gone are the days when everyone had a Beginners, Primary, and Junior Department.

One reason for the changes in departmental organization is an awareness that boys and girls do learn more quickly and with greater interest when they are grouped with children having similar capacities and abilities. There *is* a difference between the child just entering the first grade and the child just entering the third grade. Teachers who have had first, second, and third graders in the same class are keenly aware of the problems this age range creates.

Another reason for changes in grading, particularly in the preschool departments, is the growth stimulated by children's participation in public or private nursery and kindergarten programs. Normally the difference between the three- and the five-year-old is great, but when this difference is increased by the five-year-old's attendance at kindergarten, the social and intellectual contrast is startling.

Still another reason for the changes occurring in the organization of the children's division is the population explosion. Once upon a time many churches could have a primary class, including grades one through three, and hold the average attendance to under twelve. Today this is no longer possible in many many communities. Thirty or more children may be registered for a single grade.

There are also a good number of churches with a small attendance in the children's division and little hope of changing this picture in the immediate future. Rural churches and inner-city churches are frequently in this situation. Such churches, too, have a need to group boys and girls in the way that will promote the most stimulating program for children and leaders.

As a result of these developments and situations, several possible plans are offered for class and departmental grouping. Many denominations recommend at least three and urge the local church to adopt the one that is best for its particular situation. Resource and curriculum materials are usually developed with a variety of grade combinations in mind.

Here are some of the most frequently used plans:

The Closely Graded Program. This has been in existence for a number of years and follows closely the most widely used public school plan for grading. In the children's division, the Closely Graded program has the following structure, with curriculum guidance and materials for each age or grade:

PRESCHOOL YEARS	SCHOOL YEARS
NURSERY DEPARTMENT	PRIMARY DEPARTMENT
Nursery Home Roll	*Grade I*
Two-Year-Olds	*Grade II*
Three-Year-Olds	*Grade III*
KINDERGARTEN DEPARTMENT	JUNIOR DEPARTMENT
Four-Year-Olds	*Grade IV*
Five-Year-Olds	*Grade V*
	Grade VI

The Group-Graded Program. Some of the more interesting changes and developments have occurred within this program. Originally, the group-graded plan in the children's division provided for:

PRESCHOOL YEARS	SCHOOL YEARS
Nursery Class: Three-year-olds	*Primary Class:* First, second, and third grades
Kindergarten Class: Four-and-five-year-olds	*Junior Class:* Fourth, fifth, and sixth grades

The Modified Group-Graded Program. This is one of the more popular innovations in the Group-Graded Plan:

PRESCHOOL YEARS

Nursery Class: Children who will be entering the first grade in four or three years. These may be divided into Nursery II (children entering the first grade in four years) and Nursery I (children entering the first grade in three years.)

Kindergarten Class: Children who will be entering the first grade in two or one years. These may be divided into Kindergarten II (those who will be first-graders in two years) and Kindergarten I (those who will be first-graders in one year.)

Under this plan the preschool division may be either group-graded with two ages meeting together in the nursery and kindergarten or closely graded with a separate program for each of the four ages of children. The central idea is the plan for grouping the children on the basis of the time when they enter the first grade in public school.

SCHOOL YEARS

Primary Class: Elementary Grades I and II. (This group may be called "Elementary I and II.")

Upper Primary, Lower Junior or Middle Class: Elementary Grades III and IV. (This group may be called "Elementary III and IV.")

Junior Class: Elementary Grades V and VI. (This group may be called "Elementary V and VI.")

In small church schools, a broader age range of children must often be brought together. Two classes may be planned for the children's division, a preschool group that often includes first-graders, and a group for older children.

Mission study that is included in the ongoing Sunday church school program usually takes place in the regular Sunday church school groups. However, at other times the study groups may be organized on a different basis. For example, a church that has a Closely Graded program on Sunday morning may adopt a Group-Graded plan for a Sunday Evening School of Missions, placing first- and second-graders in one class, third- and fourth-graders in another, and the fifth- and sixth-grade children in a third.

Whatever the plan adopted, it is always possible to regroup children when this is justified. For example, children from the third through sixth grades may be brought together to see a moving picture and then divided into small sub-groups for learning activities best carried on when fewer children work together.

Mission education that focuses on the person's outreach into the larger community and the world has a limited place in the preschool departments. The reason for this is the limited capacity of this age child to understand events beyond the present and outside the boundaries of his immediate neighborhood. Consequently both denominational and interdenominational programs usually begin with the school-age child. However, churches may have groups for nursery and kindergarten children during a school of missions, particularly a school that emphasizes family participation. When this is the case, the total attendance, the purpose the church has for the groups, and the age range of the children will determine what grading plan is used.

In every situation, it is important to remember that there is nothing sacred about a particular grading plan. Denominational and interdenominational leaders recommend those that are best for the boys and girls in the churches. The basic reason for every plan is the creation of a situation in which children can learn and teachers can teach. Grading that makes it difficult for teachers and that puts obstacles in the way of children's learning should be studied and changed. This is one responsibility of the group that plans mission education in the local church.

PROGRAMMING FOR MISSION EDUCATION

In recent years Sunday church school curriculum programs have placed a strong emphasis upon mission education. Local church leaders, not familiar with the total curriculum content, may be unaware of how strong this emphasis is. Mission education has been included in units on the Bible, in studies of the history and meaning of the church, and in stewardship sessions. Most curriculum programs also include units that are explicitly on the world church, mission program and leaders, and the meaning of mission in the church today.

There is a reason for this emphasis, a biblical and theological reason that goes back to the nature of the church. If the Christian church is God's representative in human life and history, if the purpose of its educational programs is to help its members be mature and effective representatives, then mission education will have a central place in any curriculum program of Christian education in the Sunday church school.

Mission education is, however, also included in other educational programs.

Vacation Church School. The longer time available for each session and the shorter periods of time between sessions make the vacation church school one of the most effective educational programs of the church. Mission study units are frequently used in vacation church schools, which offer time for field trips, projects, and other activities that help children grow in their understanding of and commitment to the Christian mission.

Camps. In the intimate fellowship of camp living, Christians from overseas who are members of the camp family, can share their faith with boys and girls. Through these and other camping experiences, children may receive an informal but very effective training for witness.

Schools of Missions. These are usually scheduled at other than the regular Sunday church school period and include classes for children, young people, and adults. The interdenominational courses prepared by the Department of Education for Mission of the National Council of Churches (Friendship Press) may be used as well as denominational materials. Schools of Missions offer an opportunity for children to think and learn about some specific aspect of the mission of the church.

Family Night Programs. Often a church family night will center around a mission or world church theme. Activities are planned for age groups and family units. The program may include a fellowship time of songs and games as well as activities and a chance to gain more information about the subject selected as a theme. For example, a typical family night program may schedule:

A potluck supper followed by songs and games from other lands in which the entire family joins.

A motion picture, filmstrip, or short talk by someone who has been active in some aspect of the church's mission; or group programs for children, young people, and adults.

A worship service led by a family celebrating the unity of the world church.

Mission Study Groups. These may be planned for several departments in the children's division or for one or two classes. They are usually held on weekdays or Sunday evenings. The curriculum may be denominational, based on materials prepared for the interdenominational study theme, or a theme that has special significance for a local church. In one church celebrating its hundredth anniversary, mission study groups were organized to help the boys and girls understand the mission work undertaken on the American frontier out of which their own church came into existence, and to think about the frontiers on which God is calling them to serve, one hundred years later.

Sunday Evening Groups. Churches may have Sunday evening programs for children which supplement what is done in other groups. The curriculum materials may focus on mission study themes. Some churches plan periodic Sunday evening sessions for all ages from kindergarten up, with each age concentrating on a different aspect of a common theme.

Additional Sessions. Additional sessions are usually part of a Sunday morning program, although not necessarily so. What is studied is different from, but supplements, the Sunday church school curriculum. Mission study units may be used.

Weekday Religious Education. Released time and other weekday programs may center on the world outreach of the Christian church, mission frontiers, or other mission education concerns. Weekday religious education is most frequently interdenominational in sponsorship and leadership.

Children's Choirs. Music is a common possession of the world church, and the songs that are sung by Christians around the world symbolize the unity of the church in faith and work. Boys and girls grow in their appreciation for the church and their sense of relationship to it through learning songs and hymns that are sung by children in other lands. Children's choirs have an important function in mission education. The choir leaders are in a position to help children not only understand and appreciate the music they are learning but also to become familiar with the situations out of which songs and hymns have come and the meaning they have in the lives of the people who created them.

Few churches can make use of all of these means for mission education. Most churches will emphasize what is included in the Sunday church school curriculum and the annual denominational and interdenominational mission study theme. The latter may be pursued in several of the groups mentioned and is frequently used in schools of missions and mission study groups.

In addition to the planned and scheduled groups mentioned, teachers and members of the general committee need to be alert to other opportunities for mission education, including the use of denominational mission leaders and special speakers who have skill in talking to children, community and TV programs with a message for the church's mission, and current needs that the church can meet. Often these are the occasions for some of the most significant learning in the children's division because they help boys and girls relate what they learn in the church to the world outside the church—the world in which the mission of the church is carried out.

PLANNING MISSION EDUCATION
IN THE CURRICULUM

The word *curriculum* is used to mean a number of different things, but in Christian and mission education, curriculum refers to the *planned program* of the church through which its members are stimulated to grow in their Christian faith and witness. Specific lesson materials, the activities that are planned through which learning is encouraged, the human and physical environment in which the materials are used are all part of curriculum in every teaching-learning situation.

Lesson Materials. Lesson materials may be thought of in two categories: the basic materials planned for a teaching-learning unit and the supplementary resources used to strengthen and enrich the teaching of the unit. Both are known as curriculum materials.

Mission education curriculum materials are prepared by denominations for use in their own churches. Often these emphasize the mission leadership, work, and interests of the denomination producing the materials. The denominational materials include units in the Sunday church school program, units for Vacation Church School use, for Schools of Missions, and for mission study groups. Units may also be prepared for additional sessions of the Sunday church school.

In addition to these units of study, denominations produce many types of supplementary resources, including bulletins and leaflets on specific mission work and missionary leadership; pictures and maps; filmstrips, recordings, and motion pictures; articles for leaders' magazines and for children's story papers; interpretations of projects through which children may actively participate in the mission of their church.

A local church may learn what its own denomination has available by writing to its Board of Christian Education, Board of Missions, or Board of World Outreach for information about current publications and other resources. Some churches have service leaflets listing the mission study units in the Sunday church school curriculum and the other units that are available.

Denominations working together through Friendship Press (the Department of Education for Mission of the National Council of Churches) prepare and produce units of study as well as supplementary resources. Each year, courses for primary and junior children, including a storybook for the boys and girls and an accompanying guide for leaders, are published by Friendship Press on the current mission study theme. Since these themes are also the basis for youth and adult study materials, the children's courses are a means through which boys and girls can participate in a mission study program involving all ages in their church.

The Department of Education for Mission (or Friendship Press), also produces supplementary resources, including maps; picture albums; songbooks; leader's texts on such subjects as the use of drama, games, and activities in missionary education; filmstrips; and recordings. See page 173 for titles and types of available materials.

There is another basic resource in curriculum units planned by denominations and interdenominational groups. This is the Revised Standard Version of the Bible. It is the authority on both the content and motivation for the church's mission. All mission study units make this explicit in their content, approach, and goal.

In addition to denominational and interdenominational curriculum resources, there are sources of help from outside the church available to mission education leaders: magazines and books published by the secular press; community agencies such as museums and libraries; channels of mass communication such as radio, television, and the daily newspaper all carry information and pictures of value for mission education.

In most churches, decisions about specific curriculum units are made by the general committee responsible for mission education in the church. Teachers may secure supplementary resources through channels authorized by local churches. Some of these will be found listed in most lesson units. Suggestions are also included in the bibliography on page 173 of this book.

Occasionally a teacher will be asked to lead in a mission study program but will not be told what curriculum materials he is to use. When this happens, his best source of help is his denominational agency responsible for mission education in the local church.

The Teaching-Learning Environment. How important is the physical environment in which learning is encouraged? A moment's thought will indicate that the physical environment can not only stimulate learning but also make the teacher's task exciting and effective—if the physical environment is the right kind. A drab environment hampers teaching and learning. A rich environment provides the resources that both adults and children need and use.

There are aspects of the physical environment that concern the teacher. One is size and conditions of the meeting room or corner in which the children gather. A room that is so small that children rub elbows whenever they move, that is so dark that they must strain to see, that has drab and dirty walls, that is near distracting influences, that is too hot or too cold, makes it very difficult for children to concentrate on what they are studying.

One teacher finally gave up in despair when she found herself trying to teach a group of first- and second-grade children in a vacation church school during a hot July in a small room located on the top floor of a church building. The children were uncomfortable; so was the teacher. All the excitement of a study of India could not overcome the difficult physical conditions under which the group met. The teacher who took her place knew she could not conquer the handicap of this environment, so she changed it, and had the class meet outdoors. Physical surroundings can be a hindrance or an asset. This needs to be recognized.

A second aspect of the physical environment is the furniture. It helps to have tables and chairs that are the right height for the boys and girls who will use them, to have adequate storage cupboards, to have running water, a bulletin and chalkboard. But not every church can provide all of these. However, some items are essential. Children can dangle their legs from too high chairs and strain their backs and arms at too high table tops just so long. Then tired bodies dampen the children's interest in a program. Children are troubled by clutter and confusion.

Teachers who are blessed with well-equipped rooms can be thankful, but those who are not need not give up hope—*if* they know what they lack and have some ideas for improving their situation. Lesson materials usually provide some suggestions for furnishings and equipment. Experienced leaders in the Christian education of children can also be very helpful.

In *Friends with All the World,* Edith Welker tells of two imaginative teachers who found ways to compensate for limitations in furnishings:

One teacher whose class space was limited to the first pew in a small church found that she had no place to hang pictures. So she had the piano turned around, covered its back with soft green material, and displayed the pictures there. In another church a teacher in a similar situation secured from the local drug store a heavy advertising sign with an easel back. She coated the sign with black enamel paint and used it to display pictures. The easel was set up at one end of the pew and pictures were attached by means of masking tape.[2]

When furnishings are inadequate, the teachers' own ideas or a talk with imaginative "do-it-yourselfers" will often suggest at least temporary substitutions. However, teachers may need to start an educational program of their own directed toward the committee responsible for the church's educational ministry to children. Members of this committee may not realize how important furnishings are. Teachers can help them understand this and develop a long-term plan for securing adequate equipment and furniture.

A third aspect of the physical environment is the use that is made of the room and furnishings. This includes both the best arrangement of furnishings and their use in the educational program. One wise director of Christian education included in every training program for new leaders a session on the use of church school rooms. The potential leaders were asked to study a curriculum unit and describe how they would arrange their room or meeting corner so it would help them teach. These plans were shared, discussed, revised, and tried in actual session with children. Some-

[2] Edith F. Welker, *Friends With All the World.* New York, Friendship Press, 1954, page 81. Out of print but available in many church libraries.

times these novice teachers came up with ideas the experienced teachers in the church found very helpful, which suggests that there is opportunity for improvement in most churches.

The basic principle in arrangement is locating furnishings where they will contribute most to the program. This means that pictures and chalkboards and bulletin boards used by children must be at their eye level. It means that chairs and tables should be placed where children can use them easily. It means that areas set apart for group discussion and worship should be as far as possible from outside distractions.

One leader found a discipline problem quickly solved when he moved chairs and tables away from an open window which looked out on a busy river. Some children could not resist the temptation to watch the river and share what they saw with others in the class. When the window was not as accessible, interest in the river dropped, and interest in the class increased.

The Committee, Board, or Commission on Christian Education and the mission education group should share the responsibility for improving the physical environment in which the educational program of the church takes place. The decisions they make about meeting rooms and the efforts they make to provide adequate resources are important. Leaders also share the responsibility. They need to know what to say when they are asked what will help them in their teaching.

Teaching-Learning Activities. The curriculum materials used by leaders suggest methods and teaching-learning activities that are particularly appropriate for the age group and the content of a course being used. Usually a number are recommended from which teachers may choose the ones they feel will be of most value in their situation and of most interest to the children they teach.

However, unless the committee responsible for the overall planning of mission education in a church and the teachers who assist in the program have some understanding of the importance of methods, poor teaching may be encouraged and competent teaching handicapped.

For example, teachers may be allowed to continue certain procedures because, "I learned this way. If it meant so much to me, it must mean as much to the children I teach." This attitude can shut all doors to constructive evaluation and change.

Or teachers may be commended for using activities and teaching methods that are currently popular without anyone questioning what the children are learning from their use.

The overall committee has a responsibility for supporting teachers who are deeply concerned about the learning and growth of the boys and girls they teach, who judge the value of their work by children's progress toward the recognized goal of the educational program. The committee has a responsibility for discouraging practices that are not in harmony with this goal and for seeing that the best use is made of the curriculum materials approved by the church. This responsibility is as clear in mission education as it is in any other aspect of the church's educational ministry.

Sometimes it is assumed that all children need for the study of mission education is a table around which they can sit, a map, and a Bible. It is also assumed that if the teacher knows his subject, asks the proper questions, and receives the correct answers, there is sufficient evidence that the children are learning.

What is not considered is the attitude the children are acquiring toward the mission of the church, the feelings they are developing toward learning in the church, the degree to which the children's mission zeal and commitment are strengthened. There is too much evidence that mission education carried on under poor conditions has more negative than positive consequences to make churches comfortable. Eventually the content that is learned may be forgotten, but the negative feelings linger far into the adult years of the boys and girls. The only really effective methods are those which stimulate boys and girls to study, think, seek meanings, and make the faith and mission of the church their own.

Recruiting and Training of Leaders. Leaders in the church's mission education program for children may be recruited by any one of a number of persons interested in the children's division, including members of the regular church school teaching staff, but ultimately the general committee which acts for the church fellowship is responsible for securing leadership. It is important that at least some persons on this committee know the qualifications needed for a teacher of boys and girls. Not every person enjoys working with children and not every person is ready to teach in the children's division of the church.

Who is to be sought? Some churches develop long lists of criteria while others seem to operate on the principle that "anyone who wants to teach ought to be given the chance." Groups of children have been asked to state what they like to find in their teachers. Studies have been made by adults.

A review of some of the comments made by children and some adult studies suggest that the following qualities are essential:

• A personal commitment to the mission of the church that comes from a deep experience of God's love and forgiveness.

• An appreciation for children as persons of supreme worth and an interest in helping them learn and grow in their Christian life and faith.

• A desire and willingness to acquire the information and skills that a teacher must have if he is to be effective in his job.

It helps if persons teaching mission education have a special enthusiasm, background, and interest in this field. But it is also true that adults who meet the three qualifications mentioned will become informed, enthusiastic, and interested.

Leaders who take seriously their wish to help children learn will seek and *deserve to find* adequate leadership training opportunities. The committee responsible for the church's mission education program should do its best to see that these are available.

There are many types of training programs. These include:

Summer conferences that bring together persons from a wide geographical area and provide contact with stimulating leaders in the mission of the church, men and women with experience and records of achievement on the mission frontier. These conferences also offer training in teaching methods, as well as opportunities for acquiring background information.

Area leadership schools that give adults help in how to work with a particular age group as well as an opportunity to acquire more background information. These schools may be sponsored by denominational or interdenominational agencies.

Inservice training on the local church level that provides inexperienced leaders with opportunities to observe and work with skillful experienced adults.

One of the most fruitful sources of help for adults is often overlooked because it is not recognized as an educational opportunity. This is the Sunday morning service of worship through which men and women gain deeper insights into the meaning of their faith, the ways in which the church is called to witness today, the personal meaning God has for them and the response God asks from them.

Team Teaching. Within recent years an increasing number of churches have adopted a plan called *team teaching* which has demonstrated its value in a number of ways. Children have benefited because the quality of teaching has improved. Teachers have benefited because better use is made of their educational skills and abilities, and inservice training is possible in classes where team teaching is used.

Basically, team teaching involves a group of two or more teachers working together with a class of boys and girls, usually larger in number than an individual teacher handles alone. The teachers plan together for each session, decide how the session will be developed, and take specific responsibilities for preparation and teaching. In the actual class period, changes in the plan can be made. Well-prepared teachers are able to handle these changes with much more confidence than teachers who are not sure what they will do or how they will do it.

Team teaching provides excellent leadership training because less skilled leaders can observe and work with persons who are competent and experienced; and they have the advantage of the experienced teachers' help in trying new teaching-learning activities. For example, a qualified storyteller may tell all the stories for several sessions. Other leaders watch him in action, talk with him about the way he prepares. Later in a unit, these teachers take their turns telling stories, while the experienced storyteller assumes another leadership responsibility which may be new for him.

The clues to successful team teaching are advance planning so that each person participating knows what he is to do; faithful preparation; and responsible leadership in the session.

The following chart suggests how three teachers planned their work on a team teaching basis. Notice how each adult is involved in the events of the session, yet how the primary leadership is passed from one teacher to another. Assuming that at this point in the unit each teacher is leading the activities for which he is most qualified, what teaching skills would each of the three leaders have an opportunity to observe and to learn?

TEACHING PLAN—3RD AND 4TH GRADES

Session	Lead Teacher	Teacher 1	Teacher 2
As the children arrive	Greets children	Interests boys and girls in activity center	Works with two children on reading for worship
The Group Session	Tells the story Leads the discussion about the story and planning for activities	Sits with children	Prepares resources for activity
Activity Committees	Helps where needed Arranges worship setting	Works with one activity committee	Works with one activity committee
Worship Together	Leads worship	Plays piano	Sits with children

After the children have gone, the team meets for an evaluation and planning session or determines a time for this session.

However leadership training is provided, it is important for leaders to receive from it the help they need. This includes how to plan for and conduct a class session, learning what children are like, what can be expected of an age group. Leadership training provides help for prospective and active teachers to grow in their own faith, in their understanding of mission, in their awareness of what it means to be a member of the teaching ministry of the Christian church.

Stewardship Education. In the children's division of the church, stewardship education is often linked with mission education and directed by the group responsible for mission education. In a number of denominations, different agencies plan the program for each, but they work very closely together.

There is sound reason for this. Boys and girls, even fifth- and sixth-graders, think in terms of what is concrete. The mission of the church is identified by the specific things the church is doing to witness to the world. Stewardship education is a means through which boys and girls are encouraged and trained to use their abilities, their time, and their money for God's work.

The biblical basis of stewardship is God's promise to men that they will have the earth and its resources to sustain human life and that they will be in charge of administering these resources. But people are to use the resources of God's world in accordance with God's will, for the well-being of all God's children.

In the children's division of the church, stewardship education begins as children learn to respect themselves and value what they can do for others. Without this foundation of self-respect, children are not able to accept the importance of their contribution to the well-being of others.

Stewardship education is also based on appreciation for the world God created and the need every person has for the resources that make life possible and good—not only food, clothing, and shelter, but love, friendship, and concern as well.

As children grow older, they learn to value both the tangible gifts of things and the less tangible gifts of kindness and friendship and concern. Because these are important to them, they know they are important to others. In Christ's name they want to offer these gifts to others, meeting the needs not only of persons they know but also of unknown neighbors halfway around the world.

For example, stewardship growth in the three-year-old group may mean discovering, "I can make someone glad by letting her look at the picture book or use the doll carriage." In the fifth and sixth grade, stewardship growth may mean deciding to make a regular pledge to the church and offering to invest time and energy in some project through which the church is making Christ's love known to persons outside the church.

Stewardship education is concerned with both the motivation to give and the nature of the gift. In the Christian community the motivation is the desire to use God's gifts for the purposes God desires. The gift may be concern, money, possessions, time, energy, and most important of all, the free offering of the self for whatever use God wills.

Adults who are interested in and responsible for the stewardship education of children must be aware of the capacities and limitations of the growing child at the different stages in his development if stewardship education is to be more than training in "bringing an offering." They also need to be sensitive to the importance of the child's gift, however inadequate it may seem when compared to the gifts of adults. The gift is to be valued and respected for what it is, the child's contribution to the work of his church, given because he wants to help his church carry out the tasks which God has brought to its attention.

EVALUATION: HOW WELL HAVE WE DONE?

Sometimes local churches continue for years following the same program, secure in the belief that what is happening in the lives of boys and girls is fruitful and good. Then someone comes along who raises questions, and church leaders are startled by what is discovered. Or the questions may not be asked, and churches wake up too late. Attendance drops, leadership is hard to recruit, morale is low.

Sometimes local churches put a great deal of time, energy, and money into changing programs, but they do not try to find out how worthwhile the results of their efforts are.

Sometimes leaders attack what a church is doing in the area of education for mission, accusing the church of becoming involved in issues for which it has no responsibility or jurisdiction.

Sometimes leaders feel they can make wiser choices of curriculum materials than those responsible for the programs. These leaders want to go their own way, in some cases using resources whose point of view runs counter to the tenets of their denomination.

The group responsible for the overall program of mission education needs to be aware of situations like those described in this chapter and be prepared to take steps to handle the problems they raise. One method is a well-planned and regular process of evaluation.

Evaluation is not merely judgment and criticism. Evaluation is a means for obtaining the kind of information that can make improvement possible.

A responsible evaluation of a mission education program must take into consideration the following:

• The goals which the church seeks to achieve through what it does.

• The means—including programs, leadership training, curriculum resources, teaching procedures—that are used to reach the goal.

.• Dependable information about the degree to which the means have been effective in accomplishing what is sought.

In the program of the church, evaluation can be difficult because church groups may not be clear about their goals or the goals that are stated are not the ones really operating in the minds of teachers. It is often hard to get dependable information about class work or there is reluctance to check results, especially since what the church seeks is not easily verified by the usual kind of testing.

However, teachers who are interested in their work and who want to do their best for the children whom they teach, will try to learn the answer to: "How well are we really doing?" And the mission education committee can aid this inquiry by: 1) helping teachers know how to make evaluations; and 2) planning regular studies of the entire program.

For example, in one church following a School of Missions study of India in which classes were held for boys and girls, the children were asked to comment on the following questions:

What were we trying to learn?

Do you think you learned this? Why?

What did you enjoy most?

What are some of the most interesting things you remember from our study?

If you could go to India, what would you like to see and do?

What could Christians in India do to help us?

How can we help them?

A tape recording was made of the discussion, so leaders would have an accurate report of the children's comments.

Before the discussion with the boys and girls the leaders talked over the same questions, commenting on what they felt the children would say.

Several sessions were spent on a study of each report and on a comparison of the two reports in an effort to understand what the differences between opinions expressed by boys and girls and leaders meant. Out of this came several ideas for improving the children's programs and several that were helpful for the total church program. These ideas were incorporated in the next School of Missions and followed with a similar information-gathering evaluation procedure.

It is possible to have an effective program of mission education without evaluation, but it is hard to be sure. Sometimes leaders feel they have been miserable failures because they have not known what a class really meant to the children participating in it. Sometimes leaders have felt very successful because boys and girls appeared quiet and interested. If, in each case, the teachers had checked on what kind of learning was going on, they might have radically changed their teaching and their opinion of their efforts.

No evaluation is foolproof. Nor is it ever an end in itself. It requires planning, some effort, and a thoughtful attempt to analyze what the findings indicate. But the results can mean the difference between a successful and a disappointing experience for everyone concerned.

An evaluation period is helpful not only for individual teachers, but also for the entire local church. Where do you feel you are especially strong, and how can you maintain and build on these strengths? What changes do you feel would improve your program? Where can you take hold to get some of these improvements under way? As you call to mind your own local church situation, think about the following components of Christian education.

The Organizational Structure for Administering Your Christian Education Program. (What board, committee, or commission is responsible? How well does it function?)

Class and Departmental Grading. (In the light of alternative plans, is yours the best for your children's division?)

The Programs Through Which Mission Education Is Carried On. (Are you doing all you can? What other programs might be added?)

The Curriculum—Including Materials, Physical Environment, Teaching-Learning Activities. (What specific changes are needed here?)

Recruiting and Training of Leaders. (Is everyone helping who should be? Are some persons teaching who might better serve their church in another capacity? What kinds of training do you need?)

Stewardship Education. (What is being done? What more is needed?)

PART III

"He took them in his arms . . ."

And he took them in his
arms and blessed them, laying
his hands upon them.
Mark 10:16

6: The Nursery Child

THE NATURE OF THE NURSERY CHILD

In the nursery department of the church there is not a great deal of mission education in the usual meaning of this term. Young children are not ready to grasp the biblical concept of mission. Nor are they capable of understanding the world mission of the Christian fellowship. But children this age may acquire or fail to acquire some attitudes that form an essential foundation for all that follows in mission education. These attitudes are not learned automatically without thoughtful help, which is another way of saying that something very important needs to take place in the church nursery group.

Let us get at the nature of these attitudes by "looking in" on some fairly common experiences of "threes" and young "fours" in which learning is going on.

"Danny's Coat Is Blue." One Sunday morning the lead teacher was introducing a new assistant teacher to small groups of three- and four-year-old boys and girls. At one table five youngsters were busy working puzzles. Each child was wearing a different color, and the combination suggested a lively bouquet of spring flowers.

The new teacher thought of this and remarked, "My, you do look nice, like the bright flowers I saw on my way to church."

The children looked at her doubtfully. The lead teacher added, "Marty has a red dress and Sally's dress is green. And Ellen's dress is yellow, and Ben's coat is brown."

"And I'm Danny," the last child broke in. "And my coat is blue!"

Marty picked up the idea. "I'm Marty, and my dress is red!"

Each child with obvious enjoyment stated his name, and the color he or she was wearing.

The assistant said again, "And you look so nice, just like a bouquet of flowers!" But the children did not respond. They were back at work on their puzzles.

"What was that all about?" the assistant asked later in the morning. "I thought I was paying those children a big compliment!"

The lead teacher laughed. "You encountered one of the most delightful and most insistent qualities of youngsters this age, their new awareness of individuality. It's almost as though they were discovering the real meaning of being a separate self. Danny understood what set him apart, and clued the others on how to express it. Later, they will want to be like others. Now each one is excited by what is distinctly his own."

"That's My Church." Alan was helping his mother show his aunt and four-year-old cousin Brett around the city where Alan lived. "And that's my church," Alan said as they drove past the red brick building. "And right there's my room."

Sunday morning Alan's and Brett's families arrived together. "You go to your room," Alan directed his mother. "I'll show Brett what to do."

Brett's mother commented on Alan's attitude toward the church. "I don't know how conscious he is of our family relationship to the church," Alan's mother said. "But I am sure he feels he belongs and likes the fact that we go together. And I'm glad he feels that way."

"A Trustworthy World of People." Susan had a difficult time her

first Sunday in the nursery group. She sobbed and cried for several minutes, and no efforts on the part of the leaders helped her. Then one of the teachers said, "Susan, your mother told me where she is. We can find her. I will take you to your mother."

Susan continued to sob, but went with the strange teacher. When Susan saw her mother, she rushed into her arms. The next Sunday Susan's mother took her again to the nursery group. "If you want me, your teacher will take you to me." Susan nodded and joined some girls in the doll corner.

A few weeks later Susan saw some television pictures of hurricane damage. She was very troubled by scenes of children's rooms flooded with water and toys stranded in mud and debris. Susan's mother understood. "The storm was bad," she said. "And children lost their toys. But mothers and fathers and lots of other people took care of the children. God is taking care of them, too, through these people."

Susan's mother was not sure how much her daughter understood, but she was sure Susan felt better. And Susan, on her part, was building a reservoir of trust in people that would help her understand the dependable character of God. This trust would support her through inevitable experiences with persons who were less dependable.

"Helped to Be Aware." Sid wore the grim look of trouble when he appeared on the nursery room scene one morning. He jerked off his jacket and headed for the block corner. Charles was already there building a tall, tall tower. Sid studied the tower for a moment. Then, before anyone could stop him, he forcefully kicked the bottom block, and the structure tumbled down. A block struck Charles on the arm, which increased his dismay. One of the teachers reached the scene in a hurry.

Quickly, she put her arms around the two boys and spoke quietly but clearly. "Sid, it makes Charles very sad when you knock his tower over. He worked hard on that tower. But I think you feel badly, too, and this is why you kicked the tower."

Both boys started to cry. The teacher held them for a moment. "When we do something that hurts another person, it doesn't make us very happy. Sid is unhappy and Charles is unhappy." She turned to Charles. "If Sid is willing, can we help you build another tower?" Charles nodded. A more relaxed Sid, a less angry Charles, and a teacher went to work.

Later, in another corner of the room, Sid and several other children drew pictures of things they had seen on their way to the church building. A child asked for a red crayon, and Sid handed one over. The teacher noticed this and remarked, "It makes us feel good when someone helps us. It makes us feel good when we can help."

FOUNDATIONS FOR MISSION

What happened to the children in these situations that helped them to learn to participate in the mission of the church? The events may seem far removed from what is frequently considered mission education, but they illustrate learning that is an essential foundation for the more specific kinds of mission education to come in later years.

In the illustrations, these boys and girls were discovering their worth as individuals. They were developing a sense of belonging to the Christian community, a community to which their families were also related. They were learning they could trust the people who represented the church in their experience. And they were becoming aware of the feelings, needs, and rights of others.

The capacity to participate in the mission of the church is grounded in these learnings. Persons need to feel related to the church if they are to want to engage in its work. Trust in persons is an essential basis for trust in God, for without a personal experience of the meaning of trust, it is difficult to know what trust really is. And awareness of the needs and rights of others must be present if people are to want to share with others what is of ultimate worth and value to them, the good news of God's love revealed to all men through Jesus Christ.

Although nursery-age children are not ready to grasp the biblical basis of mission, they are not only ready for, but also in need of experiences that will help them establish their identity as persons of worth, their belonging to the church fellowship, their ability to trust, and their sensitivity to others. What can leaders who work with "threes" and "fours" do to encourage the experiences that will make these learnings possible?

PREPARING TO TEACH THE NURSERY CHILD

Become Familiar with the Three- and Four-Year-Old. Getting acquainted with these children means having a general idea of what these youngsters are like. It also means knowing the particular characteristics of individuals, for no boy or girl is a carbon copy of anyone else.

Let us look at some of the characteristics and abilities that are usually present in these boys and girls, characteristics and abilities that play a major role in determining what is recommended for a church nursery group.

Anyone who has been around a three-year-old knows he is active, yet his activity is seldom focused on one interest for very long. He is able to play with others, but he also wants to play by himself. He is an imitator, doing with toy equipment what he observes adults doing in their daily lives. He has a vocabulary that is growing rapidly, but many adult words are not understood, particularly words that point to abstract meanings and general categories. He understands the difference between right and wrong, but the distinction is based on what is approved or disapproved by those to whom he is related. He wants to be liked. Alienation from those upon whom he depends is terrifying because he senses how much he needs the care and love adults give. Yet he has his dark moments and experiences when he is mistreated or knows he has disobeyed, and the fear and guilt he feels can provoke anger and deep anxiety.

These qualities make some very definite demands on the nursery program if it is to be a program that will help this age child learn. Freedom to move about; variety in play activities; a relationship with warm, understanding adults; and opportunities to touch, see, smell, and hear are essential for this age. And leaders should provide these conditions, for both the capacities and limitations of young boys and girls are part of God's plan for growth and may not be safely ignored.

Within an environment in which these conditions are present, children can build a foundation for mission. In an environment in which too many of the conditions are missing, boys and girls may feel that they themselves are not valued, do not belong, and dare not trust or reach out toward others.

Become Sensitive to the Way God May Enter the Lives of These Children. Not very much is known about the ideas of God or the feelings toward God that are possessed by the nursery-age child. Nor is very much known about the way these children think of Jesus and the Bible.

However, some things are clear. The importance children attach to God, Jesus, and the Bible is a reflection of the importance they sense adults attach to them. A teacher who bows his head and speaks quietly and sincerely in prayer, talking with God about things that are part of a child's world, communicates to boys and girls that this adult knows God and trusts him. The teacher's joy in Jesus and respect for the Bible are also communicated by the teacher's attitude, behavior, and words.

It is also clear that children this age have a capacity for wonder that is stimulated by experiences with concrete events that are not controlled by persons. A leader tells of children watching a sunset after a church family picnic, of saying to the boys and girls, "For a long, long time, longer than we can even think, there have been sunsets, and no one makes them happen. This is part of God's good plan." The children were very quiet as the sky grew bright with color and then slowly darkened.

Another teacher tells of lighting a candle in a shaded room, of the intense interest the children showed in the flame, and of their deep silence when the adult explained, "I did not plan for fire. No person did. Fire is God's gift for us to learn to use wisely. It is a wonderful gift, for fire helps us see and helps us be warm."

The full wonder of God will not be grasped by the nursery age, any more than it can be known by the most spiritually mature adult. But God and Jesus can have meaning in the nursery department. The meaning may be simply that here are words adults feel are very important; yet many three- and young four-year-olds seem capable of associating God with events in their world that are beyond the power of any person to make happen, of understanding that persons can work for God, of sensing, if not grasping the place God has in the lives of those "who go to church"— his parents and church school teachers, among others.

The nursery child's attitude toward God and the child's feeling about him *are* important. Nursery leaders dare not assume that because children's ideas change, what they think at this age does not matter. Alert leaders, aware of this, not only watch for indications of how their children do feel toward God, but consciously plan situations in which the children may experience the wonder of God's activity in a personal way and grow in their relationship to him.

Become Skillful in Your Ministry to Children. The teacher is a key figure in determining what happens to children in the church. He is especially important in the nursery group because these children are dependent upon him for much of what occurs in the program, for help in working out problems, for "know-how" in trying new activities, for support in each new venture that is attempted. The teacher in a very special way represents the church and may have a lasting influence on how the children feel about the church. When parents report a child's eager question, "Is tomorrow Sunday?" it usually means the child has found a friend in his church teacher as well as interesting activities in the nursery program. Parents whose children are reluctant or unwilling to participate in the nursery program may face a situation in which the teacher, however willing, is unable to relate warmly to this age boy and girl.

What do three- and young four-year-olds want and need from their teacher? What qualities will help children develop the warm attachment to their church that is so essential if the child is first to anticipate eagerly what the church plans for him, and later want to share what he has found with others?

One quality is warmth, expressed by smiles, by demonstrations of affection when these are appropriate, by an outgoing interest in each boy and girl with whom the teacher works.

Another quality is sensitivity, an alertness that makes it possible to understand what is going on inside a child and to respond to this, rather than to outward behavior and spoken words alone. The youngster who turns suddenly on an adult and declares, "I hate you," is far more likely to be expressing an inner hurt than a feeling for the adult. Something has happened that the child finds too big to bear, and he storms at his world. The sensitive teacher who knows this will not add to the hurt by anger or scolding. She will communicate to the child by word and touch that she appreciates how badly he feels and how much she wants to help him.

A third quality is the capacity to respect each child for the important individual he really is. Nursery-age children need this respect very much, and the mature teacher will not knowingly try to turn any boy or girl into a duplicate of another or to compare one child favorably or unfavorably with another.

The teacher will also have enough respect to go around. No child should ever feel unwanted or unacceptable to an adult who represents the church in his life.

A fourth quality is consistency and dependability. The church fellowship should be one place where promises are kept and erratic discipline outlawed. The child who is assured he will have a turn should not be disappointed. The direction not to leave the room until parents arrive needs to be enforced, not just for the immediate physical safety of the child but also because children who discover that orders may be disobeyed are not sure where they stand. Their world becomes chaotic, and they are uneasy. Harsh discipline is not in order, but consistent upholding of sound policies is important for the child's peace of mind as well as for the leaders. The child needs to feel that his teacher is a person he can count on.

A fifth quality is the less tangible but essential ability to communicate with children this age. This involves both talking and listening to the children. Talking with this age is a skill that must be learned, most adults find. It means adopting a vocabulary which is not the same as the one used in the adult world. It means remembering what words and ideas have meaning in the rather limited experience of the three-year-old. It often means speaking more slowly than is customary and saying a lot less at a time.

Listening may be more difficult for adults than talking to the nursery age. To really listen to a child is to watch his facial and bodily gestures, to hear the tone of his voice as well as the words that are used. Listening often means supplying the context for a statement, a context that may not be immediately evident. One boy approached his teacher chuckling and singing, "We hit and hit and hit. Bam! Bam! Bam!" It took some mental agility to recognize the boy was remembering with obvious pleasure a carpentering project earlier in the session.

All of these qualities can be summed up in a sense of mission to young children, a keen desire to offer the Christian faith to them in a way they can grasp and to which they will respond. The teacher who has this sense of mission will possess or quickly try to acquire the other qualities he needs for his task.

Become Familiar with the Ideal in Physical Environment and Work to Provide It. Most guides placed in the hands of nursery leaders spell out in some detail the essential kinds of equipment and furnishings for the nursery room as well as the amount of space these boys and girls need for a good program.[3] Chairs low enough for feet to rest firmly on the floor, tables that make working comfortable, play equipment that encourages boys and girls to try out experiences of housekeeping, building, hauling, puzzle construction, or whatever is needed and of interest to members of a group, pictures hung at the children's eye level, a bulletin board low enough for the children to see easily are all important. So is space, space for the children to move around without getting in one another's way. Not every church can provide all of these immediately. But teachers who know how important space and equipment are will work hard to get the best they can for the

[3] Detailed information about furnishings and equipment may be secured from the Christian Education headquarters of your denomination.

children they teach. The right furnishings and equipment help children feel comfortable and at home, and encourage learning in the church room.

There are some resources that have particular significance and value in mission education for this age. Among these resources are pictures of the world's children engaged in activities boys and girls of every country and culture recognize—playing, enjoying experiences with their families, going to bed. The pictures which are used need to be accurate in detail and present an interpretation of persons that will encourage interest and respect.

A picture of the children's own church building is another resource. Pictures of Jesus that portray him as a person to whom young children will respond have a very important place in the nursery room. However, the number of pictures used at one time needs to be limited. Leaders should select those which remind the children of important persons and experiences, encourage conversation, and otherwise contribute meaning to a session.

A Bible that is recognized by the children as the source of information about Jesus and of other stories the children have heard belongs on a low table. Here the children may see it and touch it. Storybooks of children living in other cultures are also mission education resources.

However, the presence of these resources is only a first step. The way they are introduced and used in the program, the interest the children are encouraged to develop in them through looking, conversation, and story, will determine what the children gain from their presence. Even the meaning the Bible has for the boys and girls depends upon how it is used by the adults who are the nursery leaders.

Become Skillful in Activities Through Which Children Grow in Their Appreciation for and Interest in Their Church. A distinctive characteristic of the nursery group is freedom in and flexibility of activity. An adult observing a good program will see small clusters of boys and girls engaged in many different activities. Some may be busy with blocks and trucks. Others may be caring for dolls. Still others may be drawing large pictures, working with clay, listening to records, hearing a story. Individual children may be walking around the room just looking.

No teacher should expect to have every member of a group in one place doing one thing at one time. Occasionally this happens because the children choose to respond to an interesting opportunity, but youngsters this age who are compelled to join a large group of children for an event directed by an adult are likely to wander away unless forced to remain together. Older boys and girls are able to understand the need to work together and have the social interest and maturity that makes this possible. Three- and young four-year-olds have not reached this stage in their development.

The teacher of nursery children is present to help children enjoy an activity when her help is needed, to suggest things to do when children need her ideas, to have a rich variety of resources available for the boys and girls to use. She should also be able to stand quietly and watch, ready to be of help, but not interfering unless she is needed.

There are activities a teacher can make available to help nursery children grow in their understanding of what the church is. Visits to groups in the church, to the sanctuary where parents worship, and occasional trips to other churches to share in their nursery-age programs all contribute to the child's knowledge of his church.

Planning to share experiences and gifts with children and parents helps children understand what their church does. But a word of caution is needed here. This age child cannot really share unless he has possessed something himself, knows the other person or group who would also enjoy possessing it, and freely offers what he is sharing. Children this age do genuinely share when they enjoy something together. This may be cookies or punch at a party to which parents, friends, or other children are invited. It may be a toy or possession. When sharing includes having as well as giving, children recognize the worth of what they are giving in their own enjoyment of it.

Worship in the nursery group is important but usually brief, and often unscheduled. Through worship, the child becomes consciously aware of God who has provided many good things to enjoy and use, who plans for family care, who can help when things go wrong. Worship may be a song that is sung to celebrate a happy event, a prayer of praise or thanksgiving for food and love, a request for help when the going is rough. The content of songs and prayers should be specific: "We are glad, God, that our minister came to see us today," means more than, "We are glad for people who visit our church."

"Help me, God, not to hit Bobby. I know it hurts him," is better than, "Help us, God, not to hurt each other."

General petitions are too vague to mean very much to the nursery age. The three- and young four-year-old still lives in the immediate and responds to the specific. This child is laying the foundation for a life-long relationship with God, and it is very important that the ideas in the prayers he offers and which are offered for him be ideas he can understand. It is also important that these prayers express feelings that are genuinely the child's own.

One snowy morning the lead teacher of a nursery group told the boys and girls she had a special surprise she wanted to share with them. It was in a box. Most of the youngsters gathered around the box and tried to guess what it contained. The teacher responded to their questions: "No, it's not a puppy." "It's not cookies." "It's not a doll." When the guessing slowed down, the teacher opened the box. There, resting on some green velvet, was a yellow crocus in a small yellow vase. For a moment the children just looked. Then one boy glanced toward the snowy lawn outside the church building. He did not have to explain what he was thinking.

"This is a crocus," the teacher said. "Mrs. Blane saw it blooming in her garden and she thought we would enjoy it. She asked me if I would bring it to you."

"I know about Mrs. Blane," one boy declared. "She's sick."

The teacher nodded. "We miss her, and when she couldn't come, she wanted us to see her flower."

The yellow crocus was placed on a low table, and the children touched it gently and tried to smell it. Later when parents arrived, the crocus was pointed out to them. "Mrs. Blane found it and gave it to us," several children explained. The parents were as appreciative as their youngsters.

This incident was remembered by the boys and girls for several weeks. When Mrs. Blane returned to the children, they told her that they liked the surprise box and the flower.

Parents commented on the children's interest in the flower that grew in the snow. It was sometime later that one of the children wondered if God made the flower grow in the snow. It was at this time that the teacher offered a brief prayer of thanks for the yellow crocus and for Mrs. Blane, whose gift it was.

This illustration describes an event in the church fellowship that clearly had meaning for the boys and girls who were part of it. It is impossible to describe the content of this meaning, but certainly it included memories of a yellow flower sent to them on a snowy morning by one of the children's teachers, delight that was enhanced by the way the flower was presented, enjoyment made possible because the children were allowed to see and feel and even smell the flower. Later, the wonder of a flower that blossomed in the snow was related to God because a child thought of this, and the teacher thanked God for his lovely gift.

All of these memories became part of the children's experience of the church—a good and satisfying experience. Teachers who care enough and are sensitive enough to help children find such experiences are engaged in mission education in the nursery group. They are helping their children to belong and to want to belong to the church fellowship.

Become Aware of the Importance of Family Life. In our culture young children have many contacts with persons who are not part of their immediate family. They meet community helpers, baby sitters, neighbors. But much of each day is lived in close relationship with the adults in their homes. Because of this, the influence of family life is crucial in shaping children's feelings about the church and their relationship to it.

The attitude of parents toward the church—expressed by their participation in its life and work, the way they talk about it, the quality of their interest and support—speak clearly to the three-

and young four-year-old. Teachers who know this are concerned about what happens in the child's home.

Today's children live in many different family situations. Some children come from homes where there is one parent or there are no parents. Relatives or other persons assume the functions of parents. Some children live with adults who have indifferent or negative attitudes toward the church; neighbors or friends are responsible for the child's presence in the nursery group. Some children live in homes where parents are physically present at church events but have no real involvement in what the church is and is commissioned to do.

There are many children whose parents are deeply interested in the church and are seeking to discover the relevance of the gospel in their lives, but they have not had an opportunity to experience what is meant by the mission of the church. For them the church is symbolized by Sunday morning worship, their names on the membership rolls, "a good program." And there are children whose parents are committed to the mission of the church and who show this in attitude and activity.

Teachers of the nursery age, through informal conversations with parents as they bring their boys and girls, through home calls, and through church school registration forms can learn a great deal about the families in which their children live and about the families' relationships to the church. This information will guide teachers as they work with the minister and with other church leaders in a ministry to families.[4] Chapter 11 suggests possible approaches the teacher may use to encourage mission education at home.

The teacher is not responsible for this ministry. It is the work of the church fellowship. However, the nursery teacher is a key person in this ministry, because she knows how important the home environment is for this age children.

Become Aware of the Many Kinds of Experiences Young Children Have in the Church Fellowship. For the three- and young four-year-old, the church school nursery group is usually his major

[4] See also *Helping Your Child Grow Up in Mission,* by Juanita P. Shacklett, listed on page 174 of this book.

contact with the educational program of the church. But children have other contacts that are very important. Many churches provide child care for mothers attending morning or afternoon events sponsored by the church. In a number of churches, there is a weekday nursery program for young "fours," and in some churches such a program is provided for three-year-olds. There are family nights which may include this age child. And there are all the unprogrammed experiences, including contacts with the minister, with adults the child meets, with older boys and girls. These can leave a deep impression on the child.

Teachers of this age child, working through those responsible for the administration of the educational program, can make the importance of these influences known. Teachers can try to insure that every contact the young child has with the church whether programmed or unprogrammed will help him feel that he belongs and is glad he does.

Young children have a relatively limited background of experience against which to evaluate what happens to them. When things go wrong, their whole world is "out of joint." When they are mistreated or feel unwanted, they do not realize, "This happened today, but next time it will be different." Too many unfortunate experiences can cause damage that will take a long time to undo. And the church does not always have the opportunity to repair the broken relationships and damaged feelings that appear in the lives of its nursery-age boys and girls.

Much of the *content* of mission education has no place in the program the church plans for nursery children. This content will come later when children are older and ready and eager to learn about the mission motivation and outreach of the church. But there are aspects of mission education that do have a very important place. The motivation for witness is rooted in attitudes and feelings that can be nurtured in the nursery group; in experiences that help these young boys and girls know that they are persons of worth and importance; in experiences that build trust and confidence in the persons who represent the church to them, in teachers who are accepted and acceptable as God's representatives; in experiences that knit ties of relationship to the church; and in experiences that help these children become aware of others and of their responsibility for the well being of others.

These learnings make a sturdy foundation for education for mission. Children with this foundation are ready to move on to the opportunities the church provides for them in their kindergarten years.

7: The Kindergarten Child

Gardeners know how essential a good root system and good soil are for healthy plant growth. Roots that are strong and nourished by fertile soil make possible the leaves and flowers that are prized and enjoyed.

Children are not plants, but during their preschool years they are acquiring their own particular kinds of roots that have a lot to say about their continued growth spiritually as well as physically, emotionally, socially, and intellectually. Four root systems were suggested in the last chapter: the child's awareness of himself as a valued person; the child's sense of belonging to the fellowship of the church; the child's assurance that there are trustworthy people in the church; and the child's sensitivity to the feelings and needs of others.

These are emphasized because they play such an important part in mission education. As children continue to grow—in their respect for themselves; in their relationship to the Christian community and what it believes and does; in their confidence in persons who represent the church fellowship to them; and in their awareness of the needs and rights of others—they are laying a foundation for sincere and responsible witness. One of the opportunities open to leaders of the kindergarten-age child is the continued nourishment of these qualities in the child they teach. Specifically, the kindergarten boy or girl needs to have:

• Relationships with leaders who are his true friends—on whose affection he can count, who are dependable and consistent in their treatment of him. The child sees through pretense. He is disturbed by adults whose actions and behavior are not in line with their feelings. He needs adults who are sincere, warm, and accepting.

• Relationships with leaders who will help him be his true self and encourage independence and growth.

• Relationships with leaders who set reasonable and consistent boundaries for his behavior, boundaries necessary for his well-being and social acceptance.

• Continued experiences in the church fellowship that help him to feel he is important in his church and the church is important to him.

• Contacts with children that increase his respect for their needs, interests, feelings, under conditions that encourage consideration and kindness for others.

• Opportunities for worship and for learning about God that will strengthen the child's trust in God and understanding of who God is.

Just as in the nursery group, the physical environment in which the kindergarten child meets, the program that is planned, the other experiences that are part of the child's life in the church help leaders meet the educational needs of children.

However, mission education in the kindergarten department is not identical with what is planned for the nursery age because older "fours" and children who are five have capacities and interests not possessed by their younger brothers and sisters. Persons who have observed and studied the four- and five-year-old child remind us that not only is the four-year-old more mature than the three-year-old but also that there is continued growth on the part of the four-year-old. Let us look at some of the general characteristics of the kindergarten age.

THE NATURE OF THE KINDERGARTEN CHILD

Physically, these boys and girls are taller, stronger, better co-ordinated than their younger brothers and sisters. They also are more active. The activity of the four-year-old includes a great deal of random running and chasing which can be upsetting to adults. The five-year-old is equally on the go, but usually he has a purpose for his behavior. This urge to be active is not left behind when the child comes to the church kindergarten, and if children are to feel comfortable, their need for activity must be met.

Intellectually, this age child may have a vocabulary that includes over 1000 words more than the three-year-old uses, and his vocabulary is increasing daily. Participation in a church-sponsored or public school kindergarten introduces the children to new ideas and concepts. Trips, stories, conversations, their own explorations and discoveries broaden their horizons. The kindergarten child still needs concrete experiences in order to learn, but he is beginning to understand some generalizations. Five-year-olds, for example, can distinguish between "church people" and "church building." But distant lands and distant times involve concepts that are still too abstract for this age to grasp.

The title of the film, *The Frustrating Fours and the Fascinating Fives,* suggests the great change in personal traits that takes place during the kindergarten years. The four-year-old often appears rebellious, aggressive, moody, while the five-year-old with his great desire to please and to be grown-up is a very comfortable person to have around. However, the frustrating four is every bit as much in need of love and support as the more amiable five. Yet, because he is erratic and noisy, his world may be filled with "don'ts" and scolding. The church has a special ministry to perform to its "fours" in helping them maintain their feeling of worth and self-respect and handle the sense of guilt and alienation that is the frequent result of their unacceptable behavior.

Socially, the kindergarten age child is maturing fast. He has friends whom he now consciously seeks out. He plays well with other children. The five-year-old especially is quite able to take turns without frequent reminders, to ask for what he wants instead of grabbing and snatching for it, and to respect the property of others.

This age child watches adults and tries to duplicate the words and actions he observes adults using, often to the dismay of parents and teachers alike. Although there is a place for supervised large group activity in the kindergarten, four- and five-year-olds get along best in smaller play and work groups and need opportunities to play and plan with five children or less.

In their spiritual development these children are in an "in-between stage." They may reveal a possessive attitude toward their church and a real personal interest in what happens in their church programs. They know several facts about Jesus' life and that the Bible is where people go to learn more about him. They are able to associate some common events in their daily lives with the activity of God and can voice simple prayers. There is evidence that some children this age think of God as other than a physical being. However, very little is known about the real meaning God has in the lives of these boys and girls or the kind of relationship with God that is possible for them.

This is a brief sketch of who kindergarten boys and girls are. However, no child will fit this pattern exactly. There is a wide difference between·"general characteristics" and the children who are members of a church group. Most youngsters will fall below the "normal" level in some areas of their development and rise above in others. All children are affected by the kinds of help they have received from their world. Physical growth may be dwarfed by inadequate food and care. Spiritual growth is particularly vulnerable to the kind of guidance provided by adults in the child's environment.

A second caution is the need to safeguard the individual identity and unique capacity for growth of each child, not to force children into a mold they do not fit. Every boy and girl comes into the world with capacities and abilities possessed by no one else. By the kindergarten years some of these are apparent. A few children are extremely well coordinated and graceful. Others display unusual interest and talent in drawing. The vocabulary of some will be much greater than is expected of this age. And the spiritual sensitivity revealed by a number will be truly amazing. No leader can expect any child to duplicate the talents and achievements of other children nor can any two boys and girls be expected to grow in the same way at the same rate.

But generally, teachers can expect these youngsters to be active, independent, curious and eager to learn, capable of some large-group activity, and ready to move into new encounters with God.

NEEDS OF THE CHILD IN MISSION EDUCATION

As leaders think about and plan for mission education in the church kindergarten, it is important to remember that these are still foundation years when children are forming attitudes toward themselves, their church, and others that may be with them for a long time. It is also important to remember both the capacities and limitations of this age-group, to offer them all the stimuli and encouragement for growth they can use but not to expect them to acquire ideas, attitudes, and skills that are beyond them.

In the light of this, what can the church provide its kindergarten-age boys and girls that will help them grow in their awareness of the mission of the church and their eagerness to participate in it? What kind of learning is possible and appropriate for four- and five-year-olds?

A Genuine Concern for Others. At times adults have been known to express a keen interest in a mission program located several thousand miles away but little concern for home mission fields close at hand. There are many explanations for this. One explanation is the failure on the part of the church fellowship, at the critical time in the person's growth, to help him identify his own personal witness with missionary service, to recognize that what he does in his own neighborhood is as much mission as the labor of the professional missionary.

Four- and five-year-olds are ready to understand and to respond to some of the needs of persons they know. Encouraging this as part of the children's experience in the church is important in mission education.

One Sunday, some five-year-olds were putting the last pages in a scrapbook they had been working on for several weeks. Suddenly one of the children asked, "Where's Buddy?" The others looked around. Buddy was not in the room.

"He can't put his picture in the book," another child observed. "Where is he?" This was addressed to a teacher.

"I don't know," the teacher said. "Would you like me to find out why Buddy didn't come to help finish our book?"

The children nodded. "Now," one said. The teacher smiled, told the children she would be right back, and explained where she was going to another teacher.

A few minutes later the teacher returned. "Buddy is sick," she told the children. "His mother says he feels badly because he wanted very much to come today. He wanted to put his picture in our book."

"Why don't you take the book to his house?" a child asked. "Then he can put his picture in right now." The teacher knew Buddy was well enough to do this and agreed.

"Buddy will be glad to know you thought about him," the teacher added. "I think he will feel better because you did!" The children were delighted.

In another kindergarten group a well-liked teacher missed two Sundays because of illness. On the second Sunday the children were quite disturbed because she was sick so long. Spontaneously they expressed a desire to send her picture cards, telling her to "get well." Although this activity had not been in the plan for the session, the teachers present agreed immediately with the suggestion. The cards were made by the children and sent. A week later the teacher, who received the greetings, thanked the children and told them how happy the cards made her feel.

In another group an argument arose over a boy who had stopped coming to the kindergarten class. One child remarked, "Deane's not here. He won't kick our tower." Another child added. "He always wants all the blocks."

The teacher heard the conversation and realized many of the children disliked Deane because of his aggressive behavior. She also knew that part of Deane's problem was his desire to be included in the play activities but he had no idea of how to show this in socially acceptable ways.

Later in the session the teacher told a story about a boy who had no playmates because he had never learned how to play with other boys and girls. No one tried to help him learn. When he did the wrong thing such as grabbing blocks and cars, the children always said, "Go away." But they never told him why they said it. The boy was very lonely.

The teacher suggested they act out this story and see if they could think of a way to help the boy. In the little drama a child told the one who played the part of the "block grabber," "You make me mad when you take my blocks. Here, play with these!"

Another child said, "If I grabbed your blocks, you'd be mad. But I'll let you play anyway."

Toward the end of the session, the teacher mentioned Deane. An alert five-year-old declared, "He's like the block grabber. Maybe he doesn't know any better! Will he come back?"

The teacher agreed to do the best she could to see that he did.

These three illustrations suggest situations in which kindergarten boys and girls may become aware of needs in the lives of other persons, needs they can meet. In the first incident children understand and respond to a child's disappointment. In the second children discover they can make an adult happy by a thoughtful act. In the third children grow in their ability to understand and help change undesirable behavior. In all the situations adult guidance is involved, guidance that enables boys and girls to grow in their conscious concern for others.

Teachers may plan for situations similar to these. In most groups, situations emerge in the life of the class without planning. The important factor is that the situation be real to the boys and girls and the response of the children genuinely express the concern they feel.

A Desire to Give. For many years, giving projects have been included in mission education units. These projects are important because of what the gifts mean to those who receive them and what they mean to those who send them.

Unfortunately, however, there have been occasions when these giving projects have not had meaning for the children who contributed to them. In some instances adult pressure rather than children's interest carried the project along. In others children were not ready to support the particular project planned. This happens when for any one of many reasons the reality of a need is not recognized by children.

For example, in helping four- and five-year-olds learn to share, it must be remembered that needs beyond the border of the child's own world are not real and consequently not important to him, that he cannot give what he does not know he possesses, and that the desire to give must be the child's own.

A group of kindergarten children planted some flower seeds. When the plants were large enough, they were to be added to a window box in the church nursery room as a surprise gift for the younger girls and boys. The four- and five-year-olds appeared very enthusiastic about raising and giving these plants away.

But when the seeds sprouted and the first green shoots appeared, the children became quite interested in "their plants." Each Sunday they noticed how much each plant had grown. The kindergarten leader reminded the children of the waiting window box, but it became increasingly clear that these plants meant a great deal to the boys and girls who were caring for them. The children did not want to part with any one of them. The teacher did not insist, and the plants remained in the kindergarten room.

In another kindergarten group, the children baked cookies for a Sunday morning Christmas party in the nursery room. Each child had a "sample" when the warm cookies came from the oven. Later, when the time came to present the cookies to the younger children, there was enthusiasm in the "Merry Christmas" with which the cookies were given away.

These illustrations help us to see two very different kinds of situations that can develop in kindergarten giving projects. In the first, the children were not ready to give. The experience of helping a garden grow was new for most of the children. Every single shoot was recognized and watched from Sunday to Sunday. If the teacher had insisted that the children part with their plants, giving would have been painful rather than the joyous experience it should be.

In the second situation, the children were willing and able to give gladly, and their own sampling of the cookies they made undoubtedly added to this joy. They knew how good the cookies would taste to the younger boys and girls who received the Christmas surprise.

It *is* blessed to give, but the blessedness of giving is not something that an adult can experience for children. And this blessedness is the fruit of gifts freely offered. Kindergarten children do find joy in giving when they understand why their gift is important and what the gift will mean to those who receive it. Because of this, service projects in the kindergarten department are wisely confined to needs and persons the children know or know about. Later, when these same children are older, they will be ready and eager to share not only tangible gifts, but also time and energy and skills to live as God's people in a world where there is such great need for love and concern.

Awareness of Persons Who Are Not Part of His Immediate Group. Although the world of the kindergarten child is an expanding world, it still is largely limited to family, church, neighborhood, and the weekday kindergarten experience for the children who attend one. Church leaders have an opportunity to acquaint boys and girls with persons who are not normally a part of this world. This requires planning. It means seeking out people who enjoy four- and five-year-olds, friendly adults who know how to respond to children, who appreciate their activity, and who understand what is of interest to them.

An Indian student, wearing a lovely green sari, spent a morning in a kindergarten group. She played with the children, talked informally with them, taught them a game she had enjoyed when she was a child.

A Philippine girl visited another group and described how birthdays were celebrated in her home. A few weeks later, near the time of the Philippine girl's own birthday, the children invited her to an American birthday celebration in her honor. The party was warmly appreciated by the Philippine girl and greatly enjoyed by the children themselves.

A kindergarten leader had a tape recording of songs and stories made by the five-year-olds in a former church. One Sunday morning she played the tape for the group she was then teaching. When the children heard it, they wanted to make a tape of things they did and send it to the other group. During the year, several tapes were made and exchanged between these groups.

In each of these situations children became acquainted with persons they probably would not have known had it not been for their church kindergarten. In none of these situations did the leaders talk about the "worldwide church" or even of meeting people from "far away." The emphasis was upon enjoying the contacts and responding to what they offered, but there is evidence that the children really experienced some of the meaning of a fellowship that included persons far beyond their immediate group.

Awareness of Other Cultures and Ways of Living. Kindergarten children are aware of different cultures and ways of living. Television and motion pictures bring the world family into their homes, sometimes with respect and appreciation for differences, sometimes not. When the latter is true, it is fortunate that children neither remember nor believe all they see in the movies or on television. But church leaders still face the double task of overcoming undesirable impressions when these exist and of building positive attitudes toward and interest in other cultures and races. This effort needs to begin in the kindergarten department.

The best way to develop appreciation and interest is to provide personal contacts with friendly, outgoing members of other cultural and ethnic groups. This is not always possible; so stories, songs, informal drama, and audio-visuals may be called into service.

One kindergarten class enjoyed the story of *Juan and Juanita* in the series, *Little Playmate Books, Set II* (Friendship Press, 1956). The class understood how the Philippine children felt when the bukayo candy was lost and how glad they were when the package of candy was found. The teacher suggested that the boys and girls play the incident in the story when the candy is brought back by the thoughtful bus driver. The children had a delightful time with the informal play acting, which widened their horizons to include a group of children who enjoyed candy with a strange name but who were very like themselves in many important ways.

Other kindergarten groups have looked at pictures of children playing with toys, and children at bedtime, and talked about these picture-children—the fun they seemed to have, what their parents were probably saying, the stories these parents might have been telling their boys and girls. Through such activities, youngsters in North American churches learn that there are children who may not look or dress like the people they know but who like to play, who have parents who care for them, and who enjoy similar experiences.

A mother whose daughter attended a church kindergarten led by a world-minded teacher reported that she and her husband made some critical comments about the people of another country in response to current news from that part of the world. The daughter overheard her parents' comments and declared, "I know about a boy who lives there, and I like him. I'm going to see him when I grow up!"

Whether it is protecting children against the danger of generalizations, building positive feelings toward differences, or increasing the boundaries of the child's concept of the church fellowship to include more members of the human family, contacts with persons who are "different" from the ones children meet every day play an invaluable role in the kindergarten program.

A Sense of Belonging to the Church. Many churches include programs for the kindergarten age in schools of missions and other mission study activities planned for family participation. Although children this age are not ready for regular mission study units, the experience of sharing with fathers and mothers in church programs that include activities planned for them can help them grow in their relationship to their church.

The curriculum materials used are generally selected by those responsible for the program. Denominations produce some resources for kindergarten groups. Additional session units may be used; or the *Little Playmate* books published by Friendship Press (see page 174) may be the basis for the kindergarten program.

Church family nights differ from Schools of Missions and related programs in that what is planned for the program has the family group in mind. Family nights emphasize the relationship of the family unit to the church and provide activities children and parents enjoy together.

Teachers of kindergarten children not only enjoy and learn from participating in these family programs, but also have an opportunity to become better acquainted with both children and parents. Teachers discover which parents do come and which do not and the response of parents to the program itself. Teachers may also meet some parents whose children are not related to the Sunday church school and who may be encouraged to attend through the personal invitation this meeting makes possible.

Opportunities to Acquire a Religious Vocabulary. Between the ages of three and five, most children add about a thousand words to their vocabularies. By the time a child is five years old he can carry on a conversation with other children, express his wants, and talk with adults who are interested in subjects that interest and concern him.

The religious vocabulary of boys and girls is also growing. Kindergarten children are familiar with such words as God, Jesus, church, prayer, and Sunday church school, although the meanings they associate with these words depend upon the way they hear them used and the help they receive in understanding the realities to which the words refer. One five-year-old asked with great seriousness if the minister of her church were God. Other five-year-olds know that God cannot be seen, that he is someone great and wonderful who is very important to adults and to their own lives and well-being. Some—perhaps most kindergarten children—think of "church" as the building in which activities associated with the church take place. Leaders have found, however, that children this age can understand that the church is people who love God and Jesus, if the boys and girls are helped toward this meaning.

More needs to be learned about the religious words that are within the capacity of kindergarten children to understand, but our knowledge of how a vocabulary is built provides clues to what can be done.

Because words are symbols for realities, teachers can guide children into richer and more accurate definitions of the terms important in the Christian life—but only if teachers recognize that the meanings words have are acquired from experiences the children have with these words.

It is therefore essential that teachers themselves use words accurately. It is also essential that children meet new words in an experience that will help them identify the meaning of the word. For example, a teacher may say, "We are *in our church building*. This is a special building where we come to learn more about God and about Jesus who came to show us what God is like."

One group of five-year-olds learned to use the word "missionary" with some accuracy and understanding. They had the help of a teacher who had been a missionary in India. He explained that he was a *missionary* because he wanted to tell people who had never heard of God how much God loves them, how much Jesus loves them. On other occasions he explained that church people have a *mission*. This means they want everyone to know about God's love.

One Sunday morning a child in the group brought a friend to the kindergarten and announced, "I'm a missionary. I told Sam that God loved him, and Sam came to church." The other children agreed. There was much more to the meaning of "missionary" for these children to learn, but they were clearly on the way and going in the right direction.

A word of caution needs to be expressed, however. Because so much of the religious vocabulary of the church is associated with meanings that cannot be confined within a single experience or associated with a concrete reality, there is danger in introducing words whose meanings are not made clear. This can result in the often humorous but also sad misunderstandings that stay with children. It is probably wise to go too slowly rather than too fast in the use of new words. At the same time, leaders need to be aware that children this age are interested in words; they *can* learn to use words that are new to them, and it is a prime time to help boys and girls acquire the correct words for the experiences and meanings they are having.

A Growing Understanding of and Relationship to God. The motivation for mission is the desire to be God's representative to persons, to be his channel through which his saving love, made known in the life, death, and resurrection of Jesus Christ, is brought to men. If any human being is to participate in this mission, he must know God's saving love in his own life, for what a person does not know and possess himself he neither desires nor is able to offer to others.

It is clear that the all-important center in any program of education for mission is trust in God and faithfulness to his work. Leaders in the kindergarten department want to help their children mature in their personal relationship with God. Although they cannot *make* God available to their children, for the God of the Christian is the self-revealing God, they know that God is using them as his agents, that he is depending upon them to do his work.

There is much that teachers can do to help these four- and five-year-olds become aware of God, of who he is, of what he desires from his people. Through stories, songs, and conversation, children are told what others have discovered in their own experience of God. Through planned moments of worship, the attention of the children is directed to God and how he makes himself known in experiences and ideas familiar to children. Special days, such as Christmas and Easter, are occasions for celebrating in a joyous way God's gift of his son, Jesus Christ.

The use of selected verses and stories from the Bible is a means of helping kindergarten children not only learn about God but also come to know God. Often when such stories and verses are used, there are moments when it is clear that children are consciously aware of God's power and presence. Such moments are true worship, for in them children meet God. They know that God loves *them,* that he is powerful enough to help them no matter what happens. They trust God.

When this relationship to God is real, when it is nurtured and supported by the church community, the desire comes to share with others the meaning of God's love and care. This is the motivation for mission.

THE ROLE OF THE LARGER CHURCH FELLOWSHIP

Mission education has an important place in the kindergarten program. There is much that can be done and needs to be done for this age group. And the success or failure of what is attempted depends largely upon the teacher's awareness of his opportunity and his willingness to fulfill the task set before him by his church.

However, teachers cannot do the job alone. They need help, and there are some very specific kinds of help the larger church fellowship can provide.

Leaders need as adequate a physical environment as possible for their work. This includes a room that is large enough for the kinds of activities through which this age learns, furniture that is comfortable for the boys and girls who use it, play equipment through which the children can try out events and ideas in life around them, storage cabinets and shelves, and other recommended equipment. Many churches cannot provide the ideal, but when they are aware of what is best, they can try to come as close to it as their resources permit.

Leaders need teaching materials—guidance for teaching units, pictures, books, activity materials that will make a good educational program possible. Denominational as well as secular magazines abound in authoritative articles in this interest area. Denominational boards of education will suggest recommended resources and places from which information may be obtained about others.

Leaders need the support of a church fellowship which loves and cares for all its members, including its younger boys and girls. The atmosphere of this fellowship speaks to children. Indifference and impatience hurt children. Warmth and friendliness and love attract and sustain them.

Leaders need the help of a carefully thought-through program of mission education. What is suggested for children in any one group needs to be seen in terms of other events planned for them. It is here that the overall agency responsible for the mission education of children takes hold in developing a program and in seeing that this is carried out by all involved—and that all who are involved have a chance to make suggestions for the total program.

Leaders need the help of a ministry to families so that the environment of the home both supports and is supported by what goes on in the more carefully structured program of the church. It is important that parents know what is happening in the groups organized by the church fellowship. The teachers of children have a responsibility for working with parents, but they cannot do the whole job nor should the church want them to.

Leaders need opportunities for training in how to help four- and five-year-olds grow in their sense of mission. It is the responsibility of the church to provide not only training, but training that will help its chosen leaders at the points where they need and want help.

When the three-year-old first enters the nursery group, he brings with him a very limited contact with his church and the world the church exists to serve. Three years later, this child has achieved remarkable growth in every area of his life. If the church has been faithful to his needs and his potentialities, he is now ready to venture into the primary years—prepared for the rapidly expanding interests these years will bring, and the increasing problems he will be asked to meet and handle.

He is no longer a young child whose life centers in his home. Out on his own for a good portion of each day, he must make his way in the world of the school and the neighborhood, the world beyond the boundaries of the church fellowship, and that on which the mission of the church is focused.

8: The First- and Second-Grade Child

"I'm in the first grade!"

"Look, Miss Blane. My tooth's loose!"

"I wonder what those little kids are doing" (referring to the kindergarten boys and girls).

"Why *can't* I invite Ruben to church? He doesn't do anything on Sunday morning."

These are some comments from brand-new first- and second-graders in the church. Adults who observe children this age discover how rapidly they are growing in all areas of their lives, yet how perplexing some aspects of their world are to them.

Who are these children? What is the nature of the world as they see it? How does the church help them grow in their sense of mission?

THE NATURE OF THE FIRST- AND SECOND-GRADER

In some ways first- and second-graders are not very different from kindergarten children. They are still "wiggle worms" finding it difficult to remain still and to concentrate on any one activity for more than a few minutes unless their interest is really aroused.

But when their interest is aroused, their attention span does increase—often to a surprising extent.

In other ways, first- and second-graders reveal that they have outgrown their kindergarten characteristics. They are taller, heavier, stronger, and much better coordinated. Socially, the six-, seven-, or young eight-year-old is interested in others and wants very much to be liked by both adults and his peers. He is capable of developing close friendships, although these friendships may not last for more than a few weeks.

Boys and girls this age will willingly work and play together although "girl activities" and "boy activities" are becoming clearly differentiated, and most youngsters would not be "caught dead" crossing recognized sex lines in play.

These children are both dependent and independent in their relationships with adults. They like to have adults around. Yet they also want very much to do things for themselves and to try new activities. Unfortunately, they do not always use sound judgment in recognizing their strengths and limitations. Broken bones, cuts and bruises, and torn clothing are consequently rather common.

These dependent-independent moods often puzzle and disturb church school leaders who see members of their classes welcoming guidance, affection, and help one minute and insisting on going their own way the next. This is part of the process of growing up. However, this eagerness to be independent does not mean that the children must be allowed to do as they wish. Nor do children really want this kind of freedom. They know they need adult help, adult-set boundaries for behavior, adult guidance in handling their problems.

One of the most exciting characteristics of this age is a rapidly developing ethical sense. In their earlier years, children are interested in knowing the difference between right and wrong, but the motivation is primarily the desire to win approval from important adults and to escape the pain of disapproval. Now they are seeking more universal standards for behavior, standards that are more constant and dependable than the ideas and practices of individuals. As the children grow older the urgency of this interest will increase.

This is the developing conscience that requires persons to find their own valid reasons for what they do and do not do.

In the early elementary school years, children discover that there are many bases for making ethical decisions. Some people make decisions in terms of what they can get away with, or what they want to do, or what will win approval from important people.

For the Christian, the basis for right behavior is what God wants, "what I truly believe to be God's will in this situation in which I must make a decision."

First- and second-graders, in most cases, are not ready to accept this universal principle. They still require a more concrete reason for each decision. But adults can help children by emphasizing the principle and what it means. "If you take Ben's pencil without asking him, it will make Ben unhappy. God doesn't want us to make others unhappy." "When someone lies, we are never sure when he *is* telling the truth. God wants us to be people others can trust."

Leaders working with first- and second-graders in the mission education program of the church are particularly interested in this growing ethical concern, for they know the child's basis for distinguishing right and wrong will influence his attitude toward and sensitivity to the needs of others and his commitment to God. Ultimately, each person's response to the mission of the church will be his response to the questions: What is it that God requires of me? How important do I feel God's will is in determining what I desire and want to do?

Another exciting characteristic of the first- and second-graders is their interest in learning. These children are curious about their world, about the people and events who are part of it, and about themselves. They are now acquiring the skills of reading, writing, and arithmetic that make it increasingly easy for them to obtain information without having to "go through" adults or older children. Reading is of particular interest to church leaders, for with this ability first- and second-graders can "find out" for themselves. Books and other printed resources will play an increasingly important role in the church program from now on.

Adults who work with children know there is still another characteristic of this age that must not be overlooked, the characteristic of individuality. There are two important manifestations of this among younger primary children: the variations revealed by the children in their social, intellectual, physical, emotional, and spiritual development; and the evidence of unusual abilities shown by some children.

Adults will not find the typical child in this age group any more than they will in any group. Some children will be fast learners, others slow. Some will work and play well with other children. Some will prefer to be alone or have trouble relating to a group. Some will be able to produce better art work than their teachers! Some will demonstrate fourth- or fifth-grade reading ability. Others will struggle on the pre-primary level.

The important thing to remember is that each child is a person, a different person with feelings, interests, needs, and abilities that are his alone. Each child is of supreme worth to God and should be of supreme worth to his teacher, not because of what the teacher can "make him into" but because of what the teacher working with God can help him become.

THE WORLD OF THE FIRST-
AND SECOND-GRADER

Physical growth, intellectual curiosity, ethical questions, the impact of mass communication, and public school experiences open up a rapidly expanding world in the lives of these children, a world that is both exciting and frightening—the world in which the mission of the church is carried on.

With the advent of first grade, the lives of children are no longer primarily family centered and family protected. Now each boy and girl must make his own way in situations where parents are not on call to smooth out the rough places.

Each boy and girl must adjust to strange schoolroom procedures that are very different from the routine of family life, to a day that is scheduled, to a teacher who appears all powerful. Each boy and girl finds himself or herself expected to acquire skills and behavior patterns that are valued by peers. Otherwise the children experience the humiliation of being "the last one chosen," the constant loser.

One of the most interesting and sometimes most devastating factors in this expanding world is the child's encounter with ideas and points of view and behavior that question the authority of his home. The child discovers that not everyone thinks or acts or feels as his parents do.

Very often the church plays a role in this conflict of ideas and practices. Younger primary children begin to wonder about their church, how important it really is, why there are different churches. They learn that a loved public school teacher goes to a different church or no church. They wonder why. Friends may laugh at them for spending so much of Sunday in church activities or invite them to all day Sunday picnics and outings. They may be unhappy and puzzled when parents insist that church comes first. Other friends their age may be joining the church and "taking first communion," and Protestant boys and girls wonder why they cannot join their church *now*.

Very often parents figure in this conflict of ideas and practices. A child who has been taught to play with only "his kind" of children may find a friend in a different group and discover that his parents do not welcome this friendship. A child who has been encouraged to be friendly with all children may discover there is an "in group" and an "out group" in his school. In many communities this social segregation reaches down into the first grade and affects even the willingness of children to work together in a church school group.

The world of the younger elementary-age child is filled with adventure and excitement and fun. It is also filled with adjustments, puzzles, and sometimes bewildering problems. It is an expanding world, but it is also a world that focuses primarily on what these children are themselves experiencing, the events of home, neighborhood, school, and church. It is a world in which both the content and purpose of mission education can make a particularly important contribution to children.

GROWTH IN MISSION EDUCATION

Younger elementary-age children are ready for mission education, particularly if they have had a good foundation in the preschool program of the church—if they respect themselves and value what they can contribute to others, if their relationship with God is growing in depth and meaning, if they delight in their church and feel that they really belong to it, if they respect and value the rights and worth of other persons.

The increasing complexity of their own world and daily lives, the questions they meet regarding their church and their relationship to it, the problems they encounter in friendships and contacts with other children and people, their rapidly developing capacity to learn and think for themselves, their genuine interest in and curiosity about their world, all provide fertile ground for the mission education programs of the church.

Although what is planned for this age child will continue to make use of situations in his daily life, since this is the world that is most real and important to him, first- and second-graders *are* ready to think beyond their immediate horizons. They are interested in places and persons they have not seen, an interest that is nourished by school studies, by family experiences, and by their church's concern for these places and people.

Let us look at what the church can contribute to first- and second-graders through programs of mission education.

NEEDS OF THE CHILD IN MISSION EDUCATION

An Adequate Program of Christian Education. Beginning in the school years, the purpose, programs, and content of mission education become more sharply differentiated from those related to Christian education than is true in preschool education, but the interdependence between the two remains as close and important as ever. Younger school age children continue to need the best possible guidance in their total Christian growth if they are to respond to and participate in the mission of the church.

This guidance in Christian education will nourish and support the child's deepening relationship with God and his sense of being needed by God for his work; the child's deepening relationship with Jesus as the one who reveals God through his ministry, life, death, and resurrection and who makes possible the child's response to God's love; the child's growing ties with his church and his understanding of the church fellowship as those who carry the good news of God's love to others; the child's growing awareness of what it means to be a Christian and his ability to recognize that Christians are different because they want to tell about God's love.

This guidance in Christian education will also encourage the child's interest in and concern for others who are members of God's human family even when they have not accepted this membership; and his growing awareness of the Bible as the source of God's message to persons and the authority for what the church believes and does. Finally, guidance in Christian education will stimulate and nourish the child's capacity for worship, through which the child is helped to turn consciously to God in praise and thanksgiving and receive from God the direction he needs to live as God's child.

Mission education cannot be effective without the nurture of the child's life in these central concerns of the Christian faith. For the heart of mission education is the desire to share the gospel with others, and the gospel cannot be shared unless it is understood and accepted. This is why a strong program in Christian education must be the basis of all effort in mission education.

Experiencing the Church Fellowship as a Fellowship Important to Him. As younger elementary-school-age children move out into the world and discover that there are disagreements about what is right and good and worthwhile, they become critical. They begin to ask, "Why should I do this and why should I believe that?"

These questions will be raised about the church unless the church, as the children experience it, is important to them. This suggests that every leader in mission education ought to take a long, hard look at what is planned for these boys and girls in the church and ask some questions of his own: What happens here that is significant and exciting for the children who attend? Why should first- and second-graders be interested in what we offer to them? To

what extent is the real meaning of the church as a concerned, redemptive fellowship apparent to our youngsters? Is the church as
our children know it something they would want to share with
others?

Such questions bring all aspects of the church program under
scrutiny. Leaders look at their relationship with boys and girls, and
remember that teachers represent the adult fellowship to children.
Leaders look at the teaching-learning methods they use and remember the children's need to be active, their eagerness to learn,
the kinds of questions and problems they bring with them from the
world outside the church. Leaders look at the environment and ask
whether it stimulates or discourages learning, whether it is attractive or dull, filled with interesting resources or sterile. Leaders study
the kinds of programs that are offered and ask whether they support
one another or duplicate one another, whether some should be
dropped and others added.

Several mothers of younger elementary children found themselves
seated together during the social hour of a women's fellowship
meeting. They began talking about their children's reaction to a
mission study unit in the Sunday church school. Rather to their
surprise, the parents learned that all the children were deeply interested in the current study. One of the mothers summed up the
reasons for this when she said, "Pam is interested in the people
she is studying, and she was excited when a student from the country met with her group. She also likes the idea of actually doing
something with the people from that country who live right in our
town. I get the impression that all this is very real to her, not just
something out of a book."

Children *do not* believe in the importance of the church because
they are told it is important. They do learn this through significant
experiences in their own church fellowship. Something of this was
happening to Pam in the mission study unit of her class.

In a similar way, children learn that they are needed by their
church through opportunities to make contributions that count. For
a church family night, the first- and second-graders were asked to
arrange a bulletin board display on the world church theme they

were studying. This bulletin board display was seen by everyone who attended. These children *knew* they had contributed to the evening program.

During these first and second years in the primary department, it is essential that the children deepen their conviction that their church is important in their lives and that they are important to their church because they can make contributions that the church fellowship values and uses.

Thinking Through and Testing Ideas and Points of View. Although first- and second-graders are increasingly able to think abstractly and to handle generalizations, they need many, many concrete experiences and chances to test their thinking if their ideas are to be accurate, their generalizations meaningful. This principle is especially relevant in areas where there are conflicts and questions. Mission education includes the answering of such questions as: "What does a missionary do anyway?" "Why should I give money to the church?" "How do you know God loves everyone?" "Why doesn't everyone come to church?" "Are some churches right and some churches wrong?" "My father says we shouldn't tell others about God until we show that we believe in him ourselves!"

How do leaders of first- and second-graders help their children find answers to these and similar questions? One way is by a direct answer when this can be given. "People go to different church buildings to worship God and learn what he wants them to do. They do not come to our church because they like their own." "Church people have different ideas about what they do and believe. I don't think that anyone's ideas are all right or all wrong. We want to be as right as we can in our church, and we ask God to help us with this."

Another and often better way to respond to children's problems and questions is to provide situations in which children can arrive at their own answers. The surest way for children to understand what a missionary is and does is to talk with a missionary, to see pictures of his work, or best of all, to visit a missionary on the job. There are many home mission programs where children are welcome as visitors. The surest way to handle suspicion and prejudice is to help the children come to know and work with delightful people from other cultures, races, and national backgrounds.

Still another method is through conversation, planned and unplanned, with boys and girls, conversations in which children themselves do some of the talking. If boys and girls are to have ideas, they need opportunities to try them out, to put them into words. They need opportunities to consider meanings and even alternate points of view. They also need opportunities to change their minds and to receive support when they abandon a wrong idea for a sounder one. Talking with children can help them work through ideas and information that are puzzling and bewildering.

During these early school years, first- and second-graders are forming convictions about the church, about the nature of God, about themselves, and about others. These convictions may stay with them for a long, long time. It is essential that the children be helped to arrive at accurate, sound meanings that are appropriate for their maturity and stage of development. Church leaders who are alert to children's needs for this kind of help are in a position to provide it.

Learning About the Mission Work of Their Own Denomination and the Wider Church Fellowship. Children this age can begin to understand that the church is not in existence just to have church school and worship and all the other activities that take place in their own church buildings. They can understand that God wants his church people to help others, to care what happens to others. Because first- and second-graders are capable of this insight, they are ready to learn how the church responds to God's expectation.

Denominational and interdenominational mission study units are one of the most popular means for introducing children to the work of their church. Through these units, children learn that their church is helping not only in their own communities but also around the world. They learn of the many kinds of workers who, as Christians, tell others of Jesus Christ and God's love—the minister, the doctor, the teacher, those who distribute Bibles, the farmer—all who respond to people's needs and help because they know God wants them to do this work.

Through these units children may be involved in direct contact with some aspects of this mission. In a downtown church, children planned a party with a group of boys and girls from a church-sponsored community center. The party was a progressive affair, held in both the church building and the center so the children could see and enjoy both places. A group of first- and second-graders heard a Christian from another country tell how he had come to their country to explain what God meant to him and to help them learn about his church. These children were impressed by his simple account of his church and homeland. Through such contacts and study, boys and girls begin to understand who missionaries are and what mission is, because they are having experiences that help them interpret the meaning of these words and identify the words with something concrete.

Leaders who use mission study units with first- and second-graders need to remember the importance of firsthand contacts in their teaching and of valid substitutions for such contacts when they are not possible. Pictures, recordings, and informal drama are valuable teaching methods because they help to make clear and real what otherwise may be confusing and meaningless. Most mission study units include lists of recommended resources that are especially helpful in connection with the unit being studied.

Encouragement and Support of His Own Witness. Through mission education children learn how the Christian church has reached out to others with its good news and what the church seeks to accomplish for God. First- and second-graders can respond to this learning with their own witness, and it is essential that they be encouraged to do this. The witness of the church is not the property of the professional missionary who is supported by those "who cannot go themselves." It is the responsibility of all who know Jesus Christ, and this includes the younger members of the church fellowship.

Yet there is also the danger that too much will be expected of young Christians who live in a secular culture and who are particularly vulnerable to the criticisms and rebuffs that come from taking Christian witness seriously. What witness is it reasonable to expect of this age child? In what ways can he participate joyfully in the mission of his church?

Children this age can communicate their enthusiasm for their church to friends, and they can join their parents in family calls on new persons in the community. Children this age can respond to special needs. First- and second-graders have scoured neighborhoods for clothing for refugees and ransacked their own closets and toy collections when they knew children needed what they had to give.

Children this age can live their faith at the level their maturity makes possible. These young Christians have sometimes shamed adults by their ability to be friendly, honest, and forgiving even when there is great pressure to act otherwise.

Children this age can contribute to the budget of their church and to other causes because they are concerned for the people and the needs the children's money will help to serve.

Leaders who are serious about helping children experience the meaning of the church as mission will discover additional ways for first- and second-graders to witness, and it is important that children be invited to respond to all opportunities that have meaning for them.

However, it is also important that the adult fellowship—by example, understanding, and encouragement—stand by boys and girls in their witness. This age child is eager to act, to be what he believes. He will run risks and take chances, but he needs adult help and should find it in the supporting fellowship of the church.

A seven-year-old found himself in trouble when he went up and down his block inviting his friends to come to a Sunday evening mission study class at his church. The invitation was extended with special warmth to one boy who was a close friend and who was free on Sunday evenings. When this boy's parents found out what had happened they were quite angry because they belonged to a small sect that had been discouraged from starting neighborhood groups for children. It was the church school teacher who supported the seven-year-old against the disturbed parents and the bewilderment of the child's own parents, for the teacher pointed out that the boy had done nothing more than invite a friend to share in the life of his church, an invitation the minister had urged all adults in the congregation to extend to their nonchurched Protestant neighbors. The teacher's support and understanding and that displayed by other children in the class helped this boy maintain his interest in reaching out to others even though his first experience had been "under fire."

Children deserve another kind of support from their church when they express interest in including friends in their church's fellowship: a warm welcome for these friends and a program that is of real interest to the children who come. One child, after hearing the story of a mission worker who wanted every child to know and trust God, appeared the following Sunday with four friends and was disturbed by the attitude of her teacher. The harried teacher, suffering from an already overcrowded class, never expected her story to be taken with this seriousness and found it difficult to muster a warm welcome.

First- and second-graders want very much to do what is right. They want to act, and they will respond with zeal to suggestions from loved teachers and other adults. In ways appropriate for their age, they are capable of being ardent, sincere participants in the mission of the church, and they deserve the guidance, help, and encouragement that makes this possible.

Support of Their Parents. Because of their eagerness to learn and act, because of their earnest desire to do what is right and expected of them, first- and second-graders are sometimes the cause of conflict and misunderstanding between church and home. A parent's ideas are criticized because the teacher at church says something is or is not true. In the church children make friends of whom parents do not approve.

Or the reverse may be true. Parents believe their children are not gaining from their church what they should be learning. A good deal has been said of parents' criticism of church school ma-terial for its "lack of Bible." Criticism has also come for "lack of interest in missions." Children sense these attitudes and conflicts and are disturbed by them. There is an urgent need for teachers to build bridges of understanding between the church and home so that respect and confidence replace doubt and mistrust.

Personal contacts with parents are the best ways to build these bridges. Keeping parents informed of what is planned and taught —through notes to the home, enclosing the curriculum; inviting the parents to a class; and suggesting stories, pictures, songs, and other materials related to the world mission of the church for use in the home—are possibilities.

Ultimately, the goal of home-church cooperation goes beyond understanding and mutual support to a shared purpose: that both may help the children within their influence become committed Christians, active in fulfilling the work God grants them to do. But this goal must be reached by advancing a step at a time. In the first- and second-grade program there is a special need for sharing information and for building confidence through personal contacts between church school leaders and parents in the home.

THE ROLE OF THE LARGER CHURCH FELLOWSHIP

In order to provide adequate opportunities for younger school-age children to grow in their understanding of and response to the mission of the church, four elements are needed: leadership, a physical environment, a planned program, and teaching resources. The provision of these is the responsibility of the church fellowship.

Recruiting Leadership. The enthusiastic interest of this age child in what he learns, his energy, his capacity for friendship, and his desire to be liked make him a delight to teach, and adults generally enjoy working with first- and second-graders. However, the children deserve adult teachers who will understand them, appreciate their capabilities, and not abuse their trust and friendship. These are some of the qualities needed by a leader for this age. Men and women who have traveled, who have ideas, who are energetic and enthusiastic are welcomed by these boys and girls.

However, the two essential qualities of leadership are Christian commitment and a genuine interest in and desire to help these children learn. No other qualifications can substitute for these.

Mission study leaders need training for their work. Except for the material in the ongoing church school curriculum program, mission units are usually new, and every leader finds himself teaching unfamiliar content that makes heavy demands on him. Even those who have had a good deal of teaching experience are helped by training in the particular units they will use. The training should include background information on the mission area or type of work on which the unit centers, the teaching-learning activities that are recommended for use, what supplementary resources will be helpful and where these can be obtained, and what should happen to the children in the group.

Planning Teaching-Learning Activities. Field trips, audio-visuals, drama, and contacts with resource persons who know something about the material being studied, are among the best teaching-learning activities for this age. Stories, conversation, choric movement, and books such as the *Little Playmate Series* (see page 174) which the children can read themselves, are also useful in teaching. Leaders should stay away from the more abstract methods and materials such as the study of graphs, charts, and complicated maps, and concentrate on firsthand experiences.

Providing a Stimulating Physical Environment. The ideal teaching-learning environment for mission education programs planned for first- and second-graders is an airy, attractive room large enough for lots of activity, furnished with child-sized equipment; with cabinets, and shelves for books, collections, and teaching materials; a bulletin board and chalk board with space for the use of children and leaders; a piano and a record player. Many churches cannot provide this environment, but they can approach it as closely as their resources allow and improve what they have as rapidly as possible.

Making Available Teaching Resources. Materials used in mission education study for this age will probably be of three types: the units in the regular Sunday church program that are devoted to mission study and those that include a major emphasis on it; denominational units on areas or themes of current concern; and interdenominational materials prepared by the Department of Education for Mission of the National Council of Churches (Friendship Press). Information about mission study themes and materials may be obtained by studying the Sunday church school materials your church uses, and by watching for announcements of children's titles for annual theme materials in your denominational educational magazines.

Planning the Program. There are three sound reasons for planning the mission education program for the first- and second-graders with the total Christian education program of the church in mind. The first is the need to avoid duplication in content. The second is to prevent competition in scheduling. A third is to make the best use of the child's time. The latter may seem a strange concern, but first- and second-graders often face heavy demands on their time, demands from the school and the family as well as the church. They have to be protected against these demands because they are not able to protect themselves. Sometimes, too, they drop worthwhile activities because neither their strength nor the length of their day makes it possible to include them. More information about relating what is planned for this age to the total church program may be found in Chapter 5.

There are many programs in addition to the Sunday church school through which the church can provide mission study opportunities for first- and second-graders. Vacation church schools and weekday religious education may use units on missionary education themes. Usually Schools of Missions include groups for first- and second-graders. Choir groups composed of younger children often learn songs from Christian communities around the world and the situations that gave birth to these songs. This can be mission study.

From all these opportunities, each church needs to select the ones which are most valuable for its children and through which the church can do the most effective job of mission education. There is nothing sacred about any one of them, but every church does have an urgent responsibility *to see that it has a program,* and that this program represents its best efforts for this age group.

9: The Third- and Fourth-Grade Child

A group of third- and fourth-grade children were asked: "Who do you think a missionary is? What do you think he does?" The responses of the children indicated a variety of ideas and understandings: "A missionary is someone who goes to other places to talk about God and Jesus." "He reads the Bible." "He preaches under trees." "If he's a doctor, he makes people well." "He tells people how to get rid of snakes and spiders."

Although these replies are not necessarily characteristic of the age, they do reflect some of the inadequate conceptions children develop—conceptions that are not always corrected by the time boys and girls reach adult years.

These replies indicate also that children this age can have ideas about missionaries and their activities. The word "missionary" is connected with something definite in children's minds. To state this a little differently, by the time boys and girls are in the third and fourth grades, leaders can assume that they have had some exposure to mission education that has left impressions—some of which are sound, while others are of dubious value. Teachers need to be alert to what their boys and girls already think, and to stand ready to help them correct erroneous conceptions.

THE NATURE OF THE THIRD-
AND FOURTH-GRADER

The nature of the third- and fourth-grader makes this task particularly satisfying, interesting, and demanding, for these children stand "in-between" the period of earlier dependent childhood and the more mature years that lie ahead.

By the time boys and girls reach the third and fourth grades they have capacities and characteristics that make these years crucial ones in mission education, and influence what is included in mission study programs. Let us look at four of these characteristics:

Peer Loyalty and Independence. During the eighth and ninth years of children's lives, the group, club or "gang" age comes into flower. Children form close attachments, but not across sex lines. Girls join with other girls, boys with other boys, and there is frequent teasing and bickering between groups.

One of the values of this group association is the feeling of strength it gives. Children join together against adults. "All the other kids are going" and "all the kids have one" are frequently heard in homes, particularly when parents question a child's request. Boys and girls also support one another against other children and individuals. This age sometimes seems cruel in its treatment of those who are "out," who are not accepted as part of the group.

A feeling of personal independence is another value group association provides children. Eight- and nine-year-olds are wise enough to know they still need adults. They also want to make some of their own decisions. With the strength of the peer group behind them, they dare to push for their own ideas and desires, whether the issue is the kind of lunchbox they will carry to school or who is accepted as a friend.

Group life makes other contributions. Children learn from one another within the group, and they learn together as members of a group. How to get along with peers, game rules, cheating and fair play, the trustworthiness of ideas—all can be thrashed out in group arguments and discussions.

The advent of the "gang age" may test the patience and understanding of adults, but it indicates that boys and girls are growing up. It also emphasizes the need to work with group-held ideas and loyalties in any educational program the church plans.

Interest in Right and Wrong. The first- and second-graders are interested in right and wrong, in how persons can be sure they know the difference between the two. This interest grows steadily stronger during the later years of childhood. There are several reasons for this: the high standards children set for themselves, standards they want very much to be "right"; the children's increasing ability to see cause and effect operating in human relationships and so to connect an act with its consequences; and the children's intellectual curiosity that leads them to ask why, to want to understand the reasons for what they are taught.

One of the needs of third- and fourth-graders is to develop increasingly clear ideas of what is right and why, to recognize that they will not always want to do what is right, and to have help in integrating ideas and behavior. If this need is not met, children may learn to pay lip service to the Christian ethic, but live by very different standards.

Carl's Sunday church school class wanted to do something for a home mission school about which the children had learned when one of the teachers from the school spoke to the class. After a good deal of discussion, the children decided they would give all of their "Trick or Treat" candy to the school. Although the class leader had some misgivings about the value of this project, she recognized that it was the children's idea, what they really wanted to do, so she encouraged them to go ahead. The plan was to meet at the church after the "Trick or Treat" calls, pack the candy to be taken to the school, and have simple refreshments.

Carl was enthusiastic about these plans and went forth eagerly on his neighborhood rounds. Before long his Hallowe'en bag became heavy, and he stopped under a street light to see what he had received. Several neighbors, knowing what the children were doing, had been unusually generous. The candy was very tempting. Carl wanted to eat some, but he knew the candy belonged to the class project. After another contribution he decided he could eat one piece. He stopped at home before he went to the church and left over a third of the candy in his room.

The candy was not missed by members of the class, but the next day Carl's mother discovered what had happened. She understood not only that Carl had taken candy which did not belong to him but also that he had faced a severe temptation. Instead of scolding or punishing Carl for what had happened, she helped him recognize that it was all right to want candy but not all right to take it. People do like candy. But, his mother pointed out, Carl knew that the candy was for other children. When he kept some he took it away from them. Carl admitted he had not felt "so good" about doing this. The conversation helped Carl to see what was right and why, and to bring his behavior into line with what he believed.

Carl, and all children this age, slip again and again, whenever the gain from the wrong action appears more desirable than the possible punishment. With help, they become more able to handle temptation. Third- and fourth-graders are very much in need of this kind of help.

Children who receive the help they need and who have the strength to live by their convictions will not ignore the tasks God gives the church to do. They will have both the wisdom and the courage to behave as they believe God wants his representatives to behave.

Capacity for Understanding Meanings. As children develop in their ability to generalize and to think abstractly, they grow in their ability to handle meanings. Teachers are able to use many religious words with the assurance that children are aware of the reality to which the words refer, an awareness that will mature as the children's experience allows.

However, this age child is still very dependent on firsthand contacts and his church needs to plan for these. These contacts and the meanings he derives from them, coupled with the guidance teachers and parents give, make it possible for the child to work out understandings of who he is and what he can do, of what the church is, who God is and what God expects of people, how to think of other people and how to relate to them, who Jesus is and what his own relationship is to Jesus.

One word of caution: Because meanings are personal, they cannot be transferred. Teachers cannot teach children what the church should mean to them, what their relationship to God should be. To attempt to do so is dangerous. The child who tries to believe what he is told may never have a faith that is genuinely his.

Interest in the World Around Him. Third- and fourth-graders are moving rapidly from a primary interest in the world of play and make-believe to a primary interest in the real world in which they live, and this world is rapidly expanding to include not only other communities but other nations and cultures.

These children are maturing intellectually. They have a memory of events and people that makes possible a more accurate sense of time and space than they had a year earlier. Their curiosity and desire to know, coupled with their reading skill, enables them to learn on their own initiative. To this growth is added the ability to understand and utilize the resources of mass communication, including programs on the social and physical sciences televised for children.

This intellectual development is evidenced in the type and amount of reading children do, the nature of their hobbies, the enthusiasm they show in collections, their questions about other lands and people. They want to know what these people do, where they live. They ask about places and events. And they are concerned about God's relationship to these people. "Does he love all of them, even those who are bad?" "Why does God let them do things we don't like?" "If God loves them, why does he let them go hungry?" "Does God have churches everywhere?"

This interest in other lands and places provides a ready point of contact between the child and the world outreach of the Christian church. However, leaders of mission study programs need to remember that a true sense of mission is not the same as an interest in the world church. It is all too possible for the latter to exist without any personal motivation to make God's love known around the world or at home. Mission study for this age, and every age, needs to keep the distinction clearly in mind.

NEEDS OF THE CHILD IN MISSION EDUCATION

A Feeling of Relationship to the Christian Community. In the preschool years, the child's relationship with the church is characterized as a "sense of belonging." This sense of belonging may not go beyond the feeling that "I like to go to church and my mother and father go, too." By the time the child enters the third and fourth grades, this sense of belonging should be identified with a group of people to whom the child feels related, who are the church fellowship for him. Except in quite small churches, children cannot know and feel related to the total fellowship, but they can have strong ties with a small segment of the fellowship where they are acquainted. And it is essential that every child have such a group relationship in his church.

Often the Sunday church school class is this group. Here children learn, worship, share questions and problems. However, teachers of third- and fourth-graders know that the class, or any group in which these children participate in the church, does not automatically become a significant group relationship for the children. The meaning must emerge from the ideas and quality of life the children find in the class.

Children this age respond to church groups in which they have a part in planning activities and making decisions on matters affecting the life of the group. They respect groups that offer them a chance to learn interesting and new ideas about the church and what it believes. They enjoy groups in which they can be active, where something is going on. They want adult leaders who are fair and frank, who try to live what they teach.

In addition to these qualities, third- and fourth-graders need a group relationship in the Christian church where they know they are wanted and welcome, where they can speak frankly about their questions and perplexities without fear of having what they say used against them, where they meet people who stand up for what they believe and who are doing worthwhile, significant things.

They also need membership in a church group where their capacity to worship will be strengthened and encouraged. Although not too much is known about how meaningful God is to third- and fourth-graders, or how children this age think of God and experience him, we know they do reach out toward God in praise, thanksgiving, and petition. They can recognize the wonder of one who provides for their care, who is concerned about their life, and who will listen to what they say. Worship has an important place in the church life of the third- and fourth-grader.

Children who find these experiences and meanings in the group relationship they identify with the church do not hesitate to offer their church to their friends. This is what happens whenever a third- or fourth-grader says to someone he knows, "Come on to my church. It's OK!"

A Theological Grounding in Mission. Third- and fourth-graders still have a long way to go before they can be expected to possess an adult understanding of the beliefs and demands of the Christian faith. But most children this age do have some basis for understanding the motivation for Christian witness. They are familiar with Jesus' life, his love and concern for persons, his dependence on God and his confidence in God's guidance; they are aware that central to the teaching of the church is the story of who Jesus is and what he did; they have experienced the church fellowship that invites people to be followers of Jesus.

Children this age also have some knowledge of the nature of God, what it means to say "God is my father and the father of others," with the Christian convictions that in Jesus Christ the world has its clearest picture of who God is and what he is like, and that people everywhere need to know God. Some children are able to think of themselves as persons who help tell others this good news of God's coming to persons in Jesus Christ.

Because children this age do have a grasp of the content of their faith and because they are eager to understand more, one of the emphases of mission education in the middle elementary years is the encouragement of this theological awareness of what mission really involves and how the child in the church is related to it.

Information About the Mission of the Church. Public school studies cover areas of the world beyond the children's own homes and neighborhoods. In the church program, third- and fourth-graders need an opportunity to learn what their church is doing in home and world missions and how Christians are witnessing in everyday life. This latter concern needs to be kept clearly in view because children as well as adults can become more excited about the unusual and distant than about mission frontiers that are familiar and close to home.

For the third- and fourth-grader, learning about the mission activities of the church and the situations in which these are carried on deepens his awareness of the motivation that makes witnessing, in whatever form it takes, an essential for the Christian.

Through the use of denominational and interdenominational mission study units, third- and fourth-graders discover how members of the Christian church serve as God's ambassadors, responding to many different kinds of needs. Children learn how these ambassadors teach, heal the sick, root out the causes of starvation and illness, and fight injustice so that the love of God may be known. Third- and fourth-graders discover what their own local church is doing, how their denomination is helping, some of the mission fronts on which their denomination works with other churches.

As children engage in these studies, it is important that the situations about which they learn become as vivid and real as possible. Field trips to places where there is mission activity, meeting persons who have done interesting work, motion pictures, flat pictures, records, and filmstrips, help to achieve this. So does the interpretation of songs, games, and celebrations from these areas. Dramatizing stories is another way to make vivid and real, persons who otherwise may be very unreal, and to help children understand the convictions that prompt mission leaders to risk and work as they do.

Identification With Persons Involved in Mission. "Identification" implies emotional involvement, concern, the feeling that "this person matters to me and I have a stake in what he is doing." This feeling is quite different from an intellectual understanding *about* persons.

Third- and fourth-graders are attracted to people who do important things, but the factors that lead a child to respond to a particular person are complex. They seem to include achievement in a field the child knows something about, an accomplishment that is respected by the child and by others whom the child also respects—including members of his peer group—and an opportunity to feel fairly well acquainted with the individual even though personal contact may be impossible.

Because there can be no excitement, no enthusiasm without emotional involvement, it is highly desirable that children become well acquainted with some persons who are doing work in the mission of the church that appeals to boys and girls. These persons should include those who lived in the past and those who live in the present—men and women, boys and girls. Some should be people the children know personally, people who demonstrate that the church is still witnessing in effective ways to the love of God, that mission did not stop with David Livingstone and Wilfred Grenfell.

As children meet these people and learn what they believe in and what they struggle to achieve, boys and girls may catch some of their spirit and become more eager to have a part in the mission of the church. They may see themselves as working with these persons whom they admire, who serve God faithfully. Identification with the life and experiences of respected persons is a strong motivation for mission activity.

Participation in Mission. The cycle of learning is not complete until new ideas, new attitudes, new behavior are lived. This is as true in mission study as it is in every other area of learning.

Third- and fourth-graders who discover what their church is doing to fulfill the tasks God gives it today and who meet people who are active exponents of the mission spirit of the church must have valid opportunities to be "missionaries" themselves.

Opportunities offered to children generally include supporting with money, time, and gifts, projects undertaken by their church;

praying that others may be helped to know God's love; inviting acquaintances to become part of the fellowship of their own church; and working with parents on family projects.

However, the mission frontier for third- and fourth-graders is not limited to these possibilities, important as they are. The minds and imaginations of children will find unexpected opportunities for witness that come in the midst of everyday life.

One weekday afternoon a fourth-grade boy found a frightened kitten on the steps of the church building. The boy knew the animal belonged to a neighbor, and although he had come to the church for a party, he carried the kitten back to its home. When the neighbor asked where the kitten had been found, the boy replied, "At the church. Maybe he knew there was a party!" The neighbor asked about the church and was impressed with the enthusiasm the boy displayed. The next Sunday the neighbor and his family attended the service. Later he told the minister, "Since we moved here this boy is the first person we met who seemed delighted with his church. We came to find out why."

In a Vacation Church School program two children wandered in from the street, attracted by the sounds of a game. They had never before been inside a church building. Members of the primary department, encouraged by the teacher, made the strangers welcome and invited them back. In their youth years they became members of the church and are now active adult leaders.

Children who discover that mission is more than supporting a project will find many ways to include persons in the church fellowship. Third- and fourth-graders are increasingly able to recognize these ways and to respond to them, particularly when they are genuinely enthusiastic about their church relationship and feel that their church is back of them and believes in what they are trying to do.

THE ROLE OF THE LARGER CHURCH FELLOWSHIP

If an adequate program of mission education is to be provided for third- and fourth-graders, some effort must be made on the part of the local church to see that the essential resources for the program are available. Leadership is primary among these resources, but leaders cannot, nor should the church fellowship want them to do the job alone. They need several kinds of help.

Evaluating the Mission Education Program. Because boys and girls this age are critical and often surprisingly thoughtful in their evaluation of what they see and hear, a church fellowship that wants its children to take mission seriously needs to spend time looking long and hard at its life and service. In its mission is the fellowship really "practicing what it preaches"? What do its activities, its budget, its program emphasize? How is the fellowship helping children become committed to the mission of the church? Do members of the fellowship recognize that non-church children in the community may be a mission frontier? In what specific ways is the fellowship witnessing to the non-Christian at home, around the world? How are children helping with this witness?

These and other questions need to be asked and answered, for children learn from their total experience in their local church. Sometimes what they observe happening outside the planned program is more lasting in its influence than what they are taught in the Sunday church school and other groups.

Recruiting Responsible Leadership. Leaders of third- and fourth-graders are never just "teachers" who meet with a group on Sunday morning or at other periods in the week. They are persons to whom children are related in the fellowship of the church, persons who can help children find answers to their big questions, who can share with children the ideas and convictions that have grown out of their own struggle for a mature faith. Third- and fourth-graders really want to know what their teachers think and believe.

Leaders of third- and fourth-graders need to be persons who understand what mission means, what it requires of people, who have some ideas about the ways the church is and should be fulfilling its mission today, and who are able to communicate this to children.

These are high standards, but they are not too high, for what they ask of the adults who work with this age group is personal involvement in their teaching and a personal sense of mission for the boys and girls they teach. Churches need to train a corps of adults who have these qualities.

Providing Resources for Its Leaders. First, curriculum materials are needed, materials that will guide teachers in their planning and materials that the children themselves may use.

Churches that group third- and fourth-graders together may wonder where to turn for their mission study courses. Some denominations publish course materials for these ages. Some prepare materials for third-graders and for fourth-graders, and a choice may be made between these, depending upon the interest and maturity of members of the group.

It is also possible to adapt either primary (first, second, and third grades) or junior (fourth, fifth, and sixth grades) material for a third- and fourth-grade class by using the more advanced content and activities if primary materials are used, or the less advanced if a junior course is chosen.

In addition to age-group appropriateness, the lesson materials that are chosen need to reflect and support the denominational program and point of view; cover adequately what should be included in an age-group program on the subject; and offer the children new insights into the nature and scope of the Christian mission.

Second, supplementary materials are needed. Third- and fourth-graders are particularly responsive to what is sometimes described as a "rich learning environment." Books, clear maps, pictures, artifacts, films, slides, filmstrips, recordings, all are of interest. Their use helps children understand the people, places, and events about which they are learning. It is important for the church to provide as many of these resources as possible, keeping in mind the need to choose those that are recommended for the age and the theme studied, and that give an honest interpretation of the reality they represent. It is as questionable to use a stereotype of peoples and places in other lands as it is to encourage overseas Christians to teach their children that the American church building looks like a log cabin and the American church leader like a television star.

Third, the physical environment is an important resource which can stimulate or discourage teaching and learning. Third- and fourth-graders do not learn by sitting still. They can listen for a time. Then they need to experiment with the new ideas and insights they have heard, and to express their thoughts in a form of their own. In order to make this possible, space is needed in the area in which the groups meet, tables and chairs that are a comfortable height for the children to use, shelves for reading materials, bulletin boards and chalk boards for posting interesting ideas and the children's work.

Overall Planning of the Mission Education Program. Many churches provide a number of opportunities for third- and fourth-graders to become familiar with and involved in the mission of the church. These opportunities include mission study in the regular Sunday church school, in vacation church school, in schools of missions, in weekday programs. Some aspect of the world outreach of the church may be stressed in children's choirs, in family nights, in Sunday evening groups. One of the responsibilities of the church fellowship is to see that the wisest and best use is made of each of the programs, and that something is planned for all the boys and girls this age who are related in any way to the church.

Periodically, each church needs to review its mission education activities, evaluating them in terms of the children who are and who are not participating, of the content, of what is being achieved, and of what else is needed. A program structure that grows out of such a periodic review is most likely to help all the children this age to whom the church ministers.

Third- and fourth-graders who have adequate opportunities for mission education and who respond to it will find themselves increasingly aware of the importance of the church in the world and in their own lives, of the urgent need people have for the unique work God entrusted to the church, of what part they can have in sharing the gospel. They also will be aware that there is more to be learned about the church and its mission, and that their continuing relationship to the church includes opportunities to find out what this is.

10: The Fifth- and Sixth-Grade Child

Sue, a sixth-grader, has many characteristics of a young lady. Her hair and clothing are neat and attractive. Her attitude toward boys is changing from indifference to frank interest. At school she studies the United Nations and has become deeply concerned about its problems and opportunities. At home she assumes responsibility for several routine household tasks. In her church Sue is interested in finding out what the church really is. She is also anticipating membership in her church youth fellowship in the near future.

Pam, also in the sixth grade, is quite unlike Sue in interests and behavior. Pam will "dress up" under pressure but prefers jeans to skirts, bike riding to parties. She also is learning about the UN in school, and like Sue is involved in this study. Pam is enthusiastic about her church activities, eager for new experiences, but not too sure she will enjoy the youth fellowship. She is quite satisfied with her present age group.

Brett, in the fifth grade, is definitely uninterested in dressing up. He is deeply involved in sports, his hobbies, and outdoor projects shared with other boys. When Brett grows up he wants to be a forest ranger and is learning all he can about the natural world.

Schoolwork is tolerated because it is required. His church interest centers around a teacher who helps him glimpse some of the important ideas for which the church stands and who shares Brett's outdoor enthusiasm. Brett feels this teacher is "OK." Brett's deep respect for the natural world carries with it a sense of gratitude for the creator of this world and a desire to learn all he can about this creator. However, he is not quite sure how the things he has learned about God and Jesus tie in with his ideas and experiences in the world of nature. Sometimes he wishes very much that he did understand.

THE NATURE OF THE FIFTH- AND SIXTH-GRADE CHILD

These word sketches of three fifth- and sixth-grade boys and girls illustrate the range in interests and maturity found in members of this age group. Most churches have Sues and Pams and Bretts among their older elementary children. Churches also have children who are both less and more mature. This makes working with fifth- and sixth-graders interesting always, frustrating at times, and genuinely rewarding, for these youngsters are especially responsive to a ministry that is planned for them.

Peer Group Interests. In addition to marked differences in maturity, children this age have a number of characteristics shared in common. A prominent one is peer group interest.

Fifth- and sixth-graders are "joiners." This is the age when girls' and boys' clubs are very popular. Children seek club relationships that offer opportunities for recognition, for accomplishment and achievement, and for learning social skills. There is also evidence that boys and girls use their group relationships as a source of strength in "battles" with adults. United, they feel more secure in resisting adult pressures, standards, and demands.

Because group relationships play this major role in the lives of fifth- and sixth-graders, the ideas and values of the Christian community are probably communicated most effectively in a group where the children feel at home and accepted and which they identify with the church. If fifth- and sixth-graders are to understand at a deep level what the church fellowship is and what the mission of the church requires, this understanding must come in a church relationship where these are experienced firsthand.

Desire to Be Productive. The individual who feels adequate, who respects the worth of his own contribution, is the person most likely to be outgoing in his interests and activities. Fifth- and sixth-graders have a great need to learn the skills, ideas, and behavior that make it possible for them to do socially valued things. In fact, the child's idea of himself seems to come largely from the response of others to what he is able to do.

To express this a little differently, if children are to feel that they can make real contributions to others, they need to learn how to do things that count in their own eyes as well as those of respected leaders.

In mission education, church leaders have an opportunity to help fifth- and sixth-graders learn the skills of service and of witness that will enable them to act effectively for the church and to stimulate further learning about the meaning and frontiers of mission.

Emotional and Social Development. The three- and four-year-old is able to understand when told that hitting or taking toys makes others unhappy. He is not able to put himself in the place of the injured child and really feel the child's unhappiness. This capacity for empathy, for entering into the feelings of others, develops gradually. The fifth- and sixth-grader has it to some degree.

One evidence of this is the reaction of the fifth- and sixth-grader to unfair treatment, whether directed toward himself or others. He is deeply sensitive to injustice and can feel the hurt of it even when others are the victims.

Because of this capacity for empathy, boys and girls can participate in the needs and sufferings of others. They can identify with others' wants, their perplexities, their loneliness.

However, leaders need to be on guard against abusing this sensitivity in children by arousing feelings that may be hard for children to control, that may leave deep hurts, or that may lead to inappropriate and unwise behavior.

Intellectual Growth. By the fifth and sixth grades children have been exposed to most, if not all of the cultural skills needed to live in the adult world, and they have reached varying degrees of competency in the use of these skills. Children can read, write, handle arithmetic problems, think abstractly, grasp the basic meanings of time and space. In some areas of their intellectual growth they have outdistanced adults—who are unfortunate enough to have been educated a generation ago—as many parents and church school leaders ruefully testify.

This intellectual development and capacity make not only the adult world but also the meanings of the adult world real to boys and girls who are aware of the tense relationships, the unsolved problems that grip the peoples of the world. Fifth- and sixth-graders are aware, too, that all is not right with the church, that it has been rejected in several areas and its representatives banned in a number of countries.

This intellectual development makes possible a theological understanding and interest that gives Bible study fresh significance. In the junior years children often raise questions about Jesus—who he is and what he stood for—which they had neither the desire nor the wisdom to raise before. They wonder about his continuing presence, the meaning of his resurrection, how he reveals God.

The junior's maturing capacity to understand, his theological concern, his involvement in the world is illustrated by the comments of two children who were discussing the atom bomb. A first-grader remarked, "If someone drops a bomb, it will go boom boom and everything will blow up. That would be one big explosion!" A sixth-grader standing nearby heard the comment and said very earnestly, "It's not going to drop. God and the UN are going to stop it. They've got to!"

To the first-grader who knew bombs only through pictures and TV, the dropping of a nuclear bomb was not a matter of real concern. For the sixth-grader, although his concept of how God would act might be questioned, the dropping of a bomb was serious business, even though he, too, had only secondhand knowledge of a nuclear explosion.

Because of the intellectual potential of the junior years, mission education is able to deal with meanings and issues that may puzzle and even bore younger children. His intellectual awareness, then, is another resource the fifth- and sixth-grader brings to mission education.

The fifth- and sixth-grader's eagerness for peer group relationships, his desire to act and contribute in socially valued ways, his capacity to feel and put himself in the position of others, and his intellectual growth make a difference in the nature of the mission education program the church plans for him. This difference influences content, teaching-learning activities, the attitude of leadership, and the emphasis on service and action included in the program.

NEEDS OF THE CHILD IN MISSION EDUCATION

A Theological Foundation for Mission. Children this age are ready to look thoughtfully into the meaning of Jesus' promise, "You shall be my witnesses," and to inquire what it demands of them. They will be stimulated by a relaxed learning environment in which they can think through what it means to be related to Jesus Christ—and where they are free from fear of judgment when honest doubts and uncertainties are expressed. They need leaders who stand ready to help but who respect the child's ideas and his struggle to achieve his own theological understanding of mission.

A problem developed in a boy's recreation group sponsored by an urban church. The problem centered around two eleven-year-olds, new members of the group, who were a very disruptive influence in the program. One afternoon these two were absent, and the leader took advantage of his opportunity to talk the situation over with the others in the group. He had his opening when one of the members remarked, "Carl and Neil aren't here, and I sure don't miss them!"

The leader responded, "They make it difficult for you when they come." There was unanimous agreement on this. The discussion continued as the boys listed all the ways Carl and Neil did make it difficult. After a moment or two the leader asked, "Do you think Carl and Neil like being disliked?" Several were sure they did. Others were not certain. One fifth-grader commented, "I don't see why anyone would, but why do they act the way they do?"

Several boys declared Carl and Neil must be stupid, and the same fifth-grader wondered if they knew any better. This enabled the leader to suggest that perhaps they really did not. How could the group help them learn? To the leader's delight, several constructive suggestions were made including "being patient while they learned the rules but not letting them get away with anything."

The leader did not press the matter further then, but the following Sunday when he had many of the same children in Sunday church school, he asked what Jesus might have meant when he told his followers to "make disciples." "To talk about him and about God," one child answered. "Is that all?" the leader pressed.

"Well," a boy suggested, "maybe letting Carl and Neil be in our group is doing it."

"Let's think about it," the leader said. "I believe there are many ways to make disciples. Perhaps we can discover more."

In this situation the leader might have said to the boys at the beginning of the discussion, "Because we are a church, it is wrong not to want Carl and Neil." If he had, the members of the group would have been far less ready to respond and far less eager to help. And they would have lost a chance to understand the theological significance of their action.

The theological understanding of mission that is possible for fifth- and sixth-graders depends to a great extent upon the training and experience they have had in the church community, their own capacity for seeing meanings in what they do, and the kind of help adults provide when children seek a relationship between the Christian faith and their own experiences. However, there are some convictions of the Christian community that have special significance for boys and girls at this stage of their development: the church is a fellowship of people charged with the task of making God's love known; Jesus Christ is an historical person through whom God is revealed; God is actively at work in the lives of people and the events of history; and God depends upon human beings to do his work. Each of these convictions has something to say about the nature of mission and each of these convictions may be used to help children understand the deeper significance of their life in the church.

A Realistic Look at the Church Today. Understanding the problems and successes of the church in the current world situation is a study that will continue into youth and adult years. It also has a place in the older elementary program. Television and news reports make it clear that all is not well with the church in many parts of the world. Some children know individuals who are barred from returning to a country because "Christians" are not wanted there. Fifth- and sixth-graders hear of accusations and charges against church leaders. To pretend that the church is successful in all its mission activities does not fool older children, and it does lose their respect. The truth of the matter is that the church has never had an easy time when it has been faithful to God's calling.

An important aspect of mission education in the fifth and sixth grades is presenting an accurate picture of what is really happening, the issues the church is facing, what its mission frontiers are, what needs God is calling his people to meet, and how they are responding.

Fifth- and sixth-graders want to know what their own church is doing and why it is doing this. Often, they will want to know why their church is not doing more, and this question, too, should be faced honestly and realistically.

Mission education for this age should include the significant achievements of the Christian community, but it should not overlook the areas in which the witness of the church has been and is being rejected. Children need to understand what has gone wrong and why. They need guidance in handling the criticisms they hear and in analyzing the problems faced by the church all over the world. They are ready to handle this material, and it belongs in their study of mission education.

Understanding of Discipleship. Children learn what discipleship means from persons who are disciples, persons who have lived in the past and persons who live today. But all too often a false picture is drawn of these persons. They are seen only in their victories and achievements. The mistakes, the uncertainties, the anxious fearful moments are not revealed. One result of this is an unreal image of these people. In the minds of children, the person who works for God is something quite other than the child knows himself to be and wants to be. If this is what it means to be God's representative, the child is sure he will never make the grade, and a great barrier is placed in the way of the child's commitment and service.

Fifth- and sixth-graders need to become well acquainted with a few people who have made a recognized and respected contribution to the mission of the church. They need to know these people in their moments of doubt as well as in their moments of great courage and achievement. Children need to know people from the present as well as from the past. Children need to meet ordinary, everyday people who are part of the children's own world, so that they may understand that faithful discipleship is possible without fame and dramatic adventure.

Children also need opportunities to consider seriously the problems boys and girls face in their witnessing and to recognize that all witnessing begins with a wish to serve God in all relationships. What difference does being related to Jesus Christ make in the way I treat my brother who may be a "pest"? What difference does it make in my attitude toward the new and "different" girl at school? What difference does it make in my loyalty to my own church and its work?

A junior mission study group learning about the church in Japan discovered that Christian boys and girls living in Japan often had neighbors who did not worship God or respect the Christian church. The Western children wondered what it would be like to live in such a situation. "Would you pray before you ate if you had somebody to dinner who wasn't a Christian?" a girl asked.

The teacher threw the question back to the class. "What do you think?" Some children said, "You should because Christians would pray if they were alone." Others said, "You would not because it might embarrass the guest who would not know how to behave."

The teacher suggested that the class pretend that they were in Japan and a neighbor who might be a school teacher was coming to dinner. This neighbor did not belong to the Christian church. "Let's act out what we would do," the teacher proposed, "if we always pray before we eat in our home."

Somewhat to their surprise the members of the class found themselves explaining the table prayer to the guest, who accepted the explanation politely, and then offering the prayer as usual.

The teacher suggested another problem. "Now suppose we are in our own home and the guest is a school teacher who does not belong to the church. Let's act it out and see what we would do."

In this situation the children did not pray. Several members of the class were disturbed and eager to justify the omission of the prayer. "We'd want her to feel at home," one of the girls declared. "If she didn't," a boy added, "we might get a bad grade!"

The teacher wondered aloud why it was easier to pray while pretending to be Japanese than it was to pray in a similar situation in their own homes. The children became involved in the real issue, the difficulty of discipleship in the actual events of everyday life.

This group did not solve the problem, but they did face it. All children need opportunities to look realistically at what discipleship demands and to measure their own strength against these demands. Children also need opportunities to practice ways they will meet and handle rebuffs and ridicule when these are encountered.

Finally, children need the assurance that the church fellowship is with them, the fellowship of adults and of their peers. Children need the support of one another, the strength that comes from shared convictions, the power that is available when people are united for an important purpose. This places a new value upon the quality of life that exists in the church peer group.

Opportunities to Plan and Carry Out Mission Activities. In their study and discussion children this age will become aware of needs in other lands and at home which are not being met, of people who have never heard of God and his love as revealed in Jesus Christ. These are opportunities through which boys and girls can extend the influence of their own class fellowship in their own community and around the world.

Some of these needs will become known through denominational and interdenominational channels. Others may be discoveries of the children themselves. One group of juniors cleaned up a vacant lot next to their church, a lot which was used as a playground but which had become littered with rubbish. The children said they did this to let people in the community know they wanted children to have "a good place to play in next to the church."

When children participate in mission service, it is essential that they make as many of the decisions and do as much of the planning and work as they can. When adults assume this authority, the project is theirs, not the children's, and older juniors are more than capable of determining and carrying through plans for their mission projects.

It is also essential that children understand why these projects are undertaken in the name of the church. The motivation is more than helping. It is the desire to share with others the reality of God's love and concern, which they have themselves experienced.

Discovering the Giving and Receiving Nature of Mission. For many years, the mission study programs carried on in Western churches emphasized the "sending" aspect of the mission in which the Western churches were engaged. The churches which "sent" had the resources, the faith, the leadership that people in other parts of the world needed. Today this situation has changed radically. Now churches in other countries are commissioning their own men and women to carry the gospel. Missionaries are coming from other lands to this part of the world to witness, and the vitality of their Christian experience does much to strengthen the Christian fellowship in the West.

Fifth- and sixth-graders need to be aware that this is happening, to hear and know these churchmen from other countries and cultures, and to value the worldwide vitality of the Christian mission.

Worship. Authentic worship is not possible without a personal relationship with God and an experience of God's presence in the time of worship. To some junior children God is the "one person who won't let me down even when everyone else is mad at me," to quote a fifth-grade girl. To other boys and girls his reality and nature are vague. All fifth- and sixth-graders need help in their growing awareness of God, regardless of the level of their spiritual maturity when they enter the older elementary age group.

The child's relationship to God is of vital concern to those engaged in mission education, for without this relationship there is no motivation to witness. In mission, children as well as adults can offer to others only what they have found true in their own experience.

Because it is primarily in worship that Christians of all ages affirm and strengthen their relationship with God and their commitment to his work, training in worship is essential for mission education. Fifth- and sixth-graders need opportunities to discuss what worship is, to experiment with worship disciplines, to develop worship materials of their own, to worship together, thanking God for what he has made possible and asking for his wisdom and strength in handling the problems and needs that are faced.

THE ROLE OF THE LARGER CHURCH FELLOWSHIP

As is true for other ages, the fifth- and sixth-grade program of mission education makes some demands of the church fellowship. The fellowship as a whole acting through its official board, committee, or commission is responsible for curriculum resources, leadership, and a teaching-learning environment in which an adequate program can take place.

Providing Curriculum Resources. Curriculum materials used with this age group may be those prepared for "juniors" or specifically for fifth- and sixth-grade boys and girls. Both denominational and interdenominational curriculum units are available for use in mission study groups, clubs, vacation church schools, schools of missions, Sunday church school, and other programs planned for this age.

In addition to the teachers' and students' materials planned for curriculum units, fifth- and sixth-graders make good use of pictures, maps, motion pictures, filmstrips, records, artifacts, and other supplementary resources. Children can provide the resources themselves, including reports from public school projects. Communities can provide libraries, museums, and often interesting places to visit. All of these make an important contribution to the mission education program planned by the church.

Recruiting Leadership. The teacher with influence in the junior's world is the person who enjoys being with him, who is able to communicate this enjoyment, who is just, knowledgeable, who has ideas, and who stands by the convictions he holds. Children do not expect their teachers to be perfect, but they do want them to be honest. Consciously and unconsciously, they regard their teacher as a representative of the church and judge the church by the adult leaders they know best.

All leaders who are asked to undertake a teaching ministry deserve training for the specific responsibilities they are invited to assume, including help in understanding the fifth- and sixth-grader, in using the curriculum materials they are given, and in understanding the place of mission education in the total Christian growth of these children.

Planning Teaching-Learning Activities. Boys and girls in the fifth and sixth grades are able to take an active part in their church programs; and teaching-learning activities that encourage this have an important place in these grades. Reports, informal drama, role-playing, discussion, map study, art and writing projects that help children gain information, clarify their thinking and feelings, and express the meanings they are finding in their study are all needed. Further information about these activities may be found in mission study units; and in *Here's How and When* and *Let's Play a Story* (see page 174).

Fifth- and sixth-graders do not need the extensive floor space required in the preschool program, but they do need a physical environment that makes activity possible. This means not only comfortable tables and chairs and room for committees to work, but also shelves and cabinets where resources can be stored until needed, wall space for displaying maps and charts and the children's own work, a discussion area, and an area that can be used for worship.

THE YEARS BEHIND AND THE YEARS AHEAD

If in the preschool years boys and girls learn that they are persons who count and that what they do is important, if they feel they belong to their church fellowship, if they believe they can trust persons in the "world out there," and if they are aware of the feelings and rights of others, they have the foundation for mission.

If in the years that follow in the elementary division of the church boys and girls continue to nurture these convictions and attitudes, to grow in their personal sense of dependence upon God and their desire to be his people, and to learn about the great task God has entrusted to his church, they are well along in understanding the mission imperative of the church.

Leaders who work with children will feel at times that their progress is more crablike than forward. This is natural and inevitable. There are periods when the growth of children is apparent. There are other periods when "nothing seems to happen." The latter times require patience and faith on the adult's part and the willingness to continue in the certainty that nothing he does will be lost, and that God's spirit is present and working with him. For leaders are not only teaching mission education; they are also engaged in mission.

When the child leaves the sixth grade and the children's division, he moves into a new culture and new age-group, the tumultous exciting world of the young person. His church will go with him, and if the church has been faithful in its teaching and ministry, the child will not leave the church. In the youth years he will learn more of what it means to be God's representative and have many opportunities to witness on frontiers that are yet to be discovered.

PART IV

"First the blade..."

First the blade, then the ear,
then the full grain in the ear.
Mark 4:28b

11: The Role of the Family
in Mission Education

It has never been easy to carry on a program of Christian teaching in the home. It was difficult in the first century, when the Christian church was very new. There was no New Testament, no graded curriculum, no fund of experience and guidance on which parents could draw. But parents did have the memories of those who knew Jesus during his historical ministry, the experience of those who met Jesus as the living Christ, and the fellowship and concern of the church.

It was not easy for parents to guide the Christian nurture of boys and girls in the second and third centuries. Now there were more written resources, but how does a parent encourage a child to believe in something which it is a political crime to accept, a crime punishable by death?

It was hard at the time of the Reformation when there was turmoil in the church. How could a parent, an ordinary everyday layman, know whom to trust, what to believe, when the church structure that had endured for centuries was condemned as heretical and corrupt? What would a father, or a mother, say to children in this kind of a religious situation?

It is not easy today, when the institutional life of the church is again under fire in many areas, when children are surrounded by a secular culture, when the conviction that Christian education is the job of the church is strong in the minds of many parents.

Yet not only concerned church leaders but wise parents, too, know that the church cannot do the job alone. Children need the environment of a Christian home if the Christian faith is to take root and grow in their lives. The larger fellowship can do a great deal, but it cannot substitute for the influence of the family.

The educational power of the home is vital in Christian education. It is also vital in mission education. Children who live in a family whose members know that God is the loving father of all persons, who rejoice in the worldwide boundaries of the Christian fellowship, who are committed to witnessing and serving in the name of Jesus Christ have resources for growth in mission that cannot be duplicated.

It is at this point that the church fellowship can help the home by awakening parents to the opportunity that is theirs and by providing the help that parents need. More specifically, the larger fellowship of the church can encourage mission education in the home by:

• Being sensitive to the problems parents face, or think they face, when contemplating mission education in the home.

• Helping parents clarify what mission education is, how it can be carried on in the home, and why it deserves an important place in family life.

• Informing parents of what the church is doing through the educational activities and programs planned for children.

• Helping parents discover their own points of contact with the mission of the church and their own ways to participate in it.

• Working with parents in an adult program of mission education.

GETTING TO KNOW THE PARENTS

Sometimes parents appear indifferent or even hostile to the suggestion that mission education deserves an important place in family life. Back of this can be a misconception about the meaning of mission education, time pressure, family interests that crowd out the church, fear of financial involvement, fear of neighborhood and community criticism, and other influences. Whatever their cause, the parent's feelings and convictions are important to him and he is uneasy or angry when they are criticized and questioned. Church leaders who convey to a parent that he does not have sound reasons for his position are unlikely to find a warm welcome for their suggestions. When a parent says, "I'm too busy" or "I leave that to the church" he will not be convinced by being told he is wrong, that he has more time or that it really *is* his job.

On the other hand, church leaders who sincerely try to understand how a parent feels and the factors that lead him to feel the way he does, who respect a parent's point of view even though they cannot agree with it, are usually listened to and heard. This is a first step in winning home support for family-centered mission education and activities.

THE PARENTS' DISTINCTIVE ROLE

There is an important difference between mission education in the home and in the church. In the church fellowship, programs and schedules are necessary. In the family, however, the prevailing atmosphere and point of view are major educational influences. What parents say and do about the church; the stewardship practiced in the home; the feelings parents express toward the world's people; conversations about current happenings in the church, the neighborhood, and the world; comments about moving pictures and television programs parents see and enjoy with children; the sense of responsibility parents have for the witness of the church in the world, all influence the attitude children develop toward the mission of the church. Often the most effective help the larger church fellowship can give parents is at the point of emphasizing the importance of the prevailing family atmosphere.

However, planned family events also have a key place in mission education, and there are activities most families genuinely enjoy which can be used for this purpose. Interest in the mission of the church can be stimulated by reading about the world's peoples among whom the church is at work; by becoming acquainted with the music and crafts of other cultures; by family trips to locations with mission significance. Some families look forward to meals when food from other lands is prepared and served. Many families have deepened the meaning of their worship together by using prayers, art, and music from Christians in other countries.

Whether the focus is on the general atmosphere of family life or on particular ways in which families nurture their own sense of mission and their knowledge of the world fellowship of Christian people, help should be available from the church. This help may include opportunities to discuss problems facing parents who want to be God's people in the perplexing world of the twentieth century, a church library from which books on the world mission of the church may be borrowed, suggestions for family projects and trips, guidance in family worship. Whatever is done, the primary purpose is to help the family become a center in which mission education is an around-the-clock experience.

KEEPING PARENTS INFORMED

A parent remarked, "They could be teaching my child Hinduism, for all I know about what happens in the Sunday School." To this a teacher responded, "And I believe we would get away with it, for all the interest parents show in what the church plans and tries to accomplish."

These comments reflect the gulf that sometimes exists between the homes of children and the educational program sponsored by responsible people in the church fellowship. It is a gulf that must be bridged, and a way to start is to let parents know what does take place in the activities planned by the church. Church leaders cannot expect parents to be interested or helpful without this information.

The most popular and widely practiced methods for informing parents include letters sent into the home describing what is taught, calls in person and by telephone to let parents know what children are learning and doing, and invitations to parents to visit children's groups in the church.

Sometimes parents are invited to special events such as a visit to an interesting mission center or to see a moving picture on a theme the children are studying. In one church, whenever the juniors entertained a guest from another culture or country, they asked their parents to meet their guest too.

Parent meetings devoted to previews of a unit of work and "open houses" at the close of a unit when children explain what they have done are also informative for the parents. When parents are asked to help with special home assignments, they are involved in and informed about the work of their boys and girls.

All the methods used to inform parents about mission education in the church need to focus on more than communicating information. Parents should be informed because they deserve to know what is happening to their children and because their support in the educational ministry of the church is essential.

AWAKENING FAMILY INTEREST IN MISSION EDUCATION

No two families are alike. Every family has its own unique identity, a style of family life that is not duplicated in any other home. Because of this, suggestions for mission education in the home that excite one family may not appeal to others.

This situation, coupled with the many, many kinds of family activities that are valuable in mission education, emphasizes the wisdom of exposing family groups to a wide variety of possibilities and letting them adopt those that have the greatest appeal and value.

The most effective exposure is a firsthand taste of what these possibilities are and what they can contribute to family enjoyment and growth. Families that have a successful time with an activity in a church program are more likely to want to try it in their homes than they are if they have only heard about it. One effective method is to plan church family nights in which parents and children experiment with various kinds of mission education activities.

One church had a "World Christian Art Festival" with an exhibit of Christian paintings and craft work by artists in different parts of the world, recordings of religious music from several cultures, and opportunities to learn songs and folk games enjoyed by Christian groups in other lands. Parents and children enjoyed the festival. The Christmas after the event, the church school gave each family a copy of one of the madonna pictures exhibited. A junior class met the week of Christmas to frame the paintings their families received. The world outlook and interest of the church was noticeably increased by the festival and what grew out of it, and afterwards many families found themselves watching for the origin of the hymns they sang and the pictures published in denominational magazines and church school periodicals.

A fourth-grade class in a large church entertained a student from another country. Parents were invited to visit the class on this occasion and to join with their boys and girls in the games and songs the student taught them. One table grace they learned that day was adopted by several of the families for their own use.

A church had a family program that included a potluck supper of dishes from other countries, a family treasure hunt in denominational periodicals to find information about areas in which the church had mission work, and a worship service in which the ties that bound them to fellow Christians throughout the world were recognized and celebrated.

In addition to gatherings that focus on the world fellowship of Christian people, families need encouragement and training in witness. A successful experiment in this area was a plan for church families to call on new families in the community. It started when a couple responsible for contacting new persons in their neighborhood took their children along when the parents were sure there were children about the same age in the families they were visiting. Appreciation was expressed by the adults in the new families who indicated that churches often welcome adults but do not always remember that boys and girls like to be welcomed, too.

However, it is sometimes at a more critical level that families need help. Parents who stand by their convictions when community pressures urge them to do otherwise can be lonely and frightened. So can the children in these families. They are ready for all the help the church fellowship can provide. In situations like these, the biblical commission to witness, the biblical understanding of the church as God's fellowship composed of those who support one another in God's work, the strength and wisdom from God that come in worship are needed. Churches dare not forget that these are central to mission education.

STRENGTHENING ADULT MISSION EDUCATION

A good argument can be made for adult education as the most effective approach to family education in the church. Certainly adults who are growing in their own understanding of the mission of the church and who are actively related to it stand a better chance of having a positive influence on children than adults who are uncertain about their own beliefs and actions. And it must be remembered that families who are outside the church must be brought in before their homes can be centers of mission education. Because this is so, all that the church does to educate its adults directly and indirectly helps the boys and girls who are related to these adults. The minister's sermon, the adult choir, home calls, adult church school classes and stewardship education, the programs of the women's and laymen's groups all help to strengthen mission education in the home.

In addition, opportunities for family witness in the community and the social and vocational circles to which families are related strengthen children's mission education. In a neighborhood where there was little play space for the children, the city had a chance to sell some land that was a popular playground. A women's group in one of the churches learned what was about to happen and organized community opposition to the move on the grounds that children had a right to a place to play. They gave credit for their concern to an adult study class on the inner city and the church.

The property owners in a suburban neighborhood learned that their area was about to become more cosmopolitan than some of them desired. There was a great deal of talk, some strategy meetings, some panic. A group of parents from several of the community churches got together, recognized the damage the situation was doing to their children, the right of every person to be secure in his own home, and the implications of the Christian gospel for the problem they were facing. They issued a statement in which they made known their position and the reason for their stand, that they did not expect everyone to agree with them, but that their concern for their children and their relationship to the church made no other position possible. One of the churches reported that two couples who felt the church had no "backbone" before this incident became active and later members of the church. A public school teacher remarked on the positive effect the parents' action had on the children. Playground arguments and peer group feuds dropped in number and intensity. The children seemed secure when they found their parents were able to handle the matter.

Whether the issue is a playground, neighbors, or another matter of community or world concern, boys and girls are steadied and helped when they live with adults who have convictions that matter to them and the courage to live by these convictions. In the lives of their parents, children see flesh and blood examples of what it means to be God's representatives in the situations in which families are involved. Adult education in the church is one important means for helping parents find the understanding and the strength they need to be God's people.

MINISTERING TO FAMILIES

There are a number of specific ways churches can help families become more alert and responsive to their opportunities for mission. In addition to planning programs that focus on family activities and interests, helping families be aware of areas in which they can witness, and providing for mission education in the adult Christian education program, the responsible board, committee, or commission in the church can:

Bring to the attention of families, and when possible, make available books, pictures, and recordings, that will broaden family interests and enable families to learn of significant mission activities and frontiers. For information about these resources, church groups may write to their denominational board or agency responsible for mission education in the home.

Help families develop their own criteria for evaluating mass media resources and programs from the perspective of the Christian mission and learn how to use these criteria in evaluating books, news stories, television programs and other communications that come into the home from the secular culture. Questions that will guide the development of these criteria include: What does the resource or program seek to do? Is this purpose consistent with the gospel? What concept of other peoples and cultures is presented? Is this consistent with the Christian conviction that God is the father of all human beings and all have equal worth and significance in his sight? What external evidence is there that the content is valid and accurate? What makes the resource or program appropriate for family use?

Help families become aware of genuine services they can render to other peoples in the immediate community and of specific things families can do to increase justice and goodwill in human relationships. One of the great needs of persons today is to feel that they can be an influence for God, that Christian witness is not futile. Many times men and women are tempted to give up because they feel they have no control over people and organizations that are making important decisions. But the Christian mission is supported by the only undefeatable power in the universe, the power of God's purpose for human life and human destiny. In an age when evil and suffering, anxiety and cynicism appear dominant, families need to recover their faith in goodwill and justice, and their confidence that what they do to establish these in human society does count.

Develop short-term study programs on current issues and problems that will help families think through the nature of their Christian witness in specific situations. Some of these groups may be for parents only. Others may include children, depending upon the nature of the problem and the approach taken by the study group. Issues that have been handled in groups of this nature include fallout shelters, school integration, social drinking, stealing and cheating, community traffic laws, church union, and support for world missions.

Families participate in the mission of the church through inviting and encouraging persons not related to the church to become members of Christ's community. Families also participate in the mission of the church through the witness of their family life, the convictions they live by, the decisions they make, the causes they support. Family members who know the strength of God's love and care speak with authority to all who wonder what they can depend upon amid the social turmoil and the international danger of twentieth century life. It is not easy to be a Christian family today. It never has been. But families who are have something vital to offer to those outside the Christian fellowship and a joy and enthusiasm in their faith that is contagious.

12: The Mission Imperative in the Lives of Children

Long ago, the author of Hebrews, writing at a time when the Christians were facing severe persecution, recalled a long line of heroic witnesses for God. He told of Abraham, Isaac, Jacob, Moses, and others who endured, conquered, suffered, lived, and died in faithfulness to their God. In his mind this author of the early church saw these people surrounding him like a cloud, strengthening him with their strength, pointing him toward the one they had not known but who was known to him, Jesus Christ.

Men and women today understand at least in part the experience of this ancient writer. They, too, have a cloud of witnesses whose faithfulness speaks to them, whose testimony brought them to Jesus Christ.

Boys and girls are surrounded by their own cloud of witnesses through whom God speaks. These witnesses may be parents whose love and physical care give them security and nourish their capacity to trust; whose understanding authority guides them through the problems they face in their broadening social relationships and their growing sense of independence; whose faith points them to an infallible God whose love is real and freely given.

These witnesses include adults who are trusted teachers; who testify by their concern and patience and interest that each child is valued and worthy of the time and energy of the teacher; and who reveal to the child their confidence in God's wisdom and care.

These witnesses include acquaintances, young and old, who are related to the child in the fellowship of the Christian church and who try to help the local church be what the church really is: God's people who serve and forgive and love, who are just and merciful because this is what God expects them to be.

As children grow older, parents and teachers and the church fellowship become a contact between the child and persons in remembered history and in the present. These men and women and boys and girls are part of the child's cloud of witnesses. They emerge from the pages of the Bible and assume reality. They emerge from the story of the church in past centuries and the present. They speak to children of what they know to be true and dependable, that Jesus Christ is the incarnation of the living God and that God alone is worthy of man's unquestioning loyalty and trust.

Slowly, as boys and girls mature in their ability to know and respond to God, they discover for themselves who God is and the wonder of his self-revelation. They identify with the church whose fellowship is unlike that of any other group because its members are bound to one another by their experience of God's love in Jesus Christ.

This realization may come very slowly for some children who are handicapped in their response to God by unfaithful witnesses, by over-exposure to the attractiveness of other values and loyalties, by careless teaching that brings uncertainty and confusion. But if the cloud of witnesses is faithful, the miracle of God's power and love in human life is seen again. A new generation comes into existence of disciples who belong to Jesus Christ and who continue the ministry he began.

This, however, is not the story of every child. Some boys and girls grow up in an environment where there are no members of the Christian community who care. From their lives the cloud of witnesses is missing. The mission of the church does not reach them.

Many of these children live in areas where Christian churches exist. Wherever they are, these children are continuing reminders to the church, that, however adequate its program may be for its own members, it is failing to be the church of God if it closes its eyes to any who are not invited into its fellowship. Every child outside the fellowship is a mission frontier. For God has entrusted the responsibility of mission to persons.

THE CHILD AND MISSION

When children are able to think of themselves as members of the living fellowship of the church, they are ready to have a part in its mission. Some boys and girls, aware of the exciting lives of missionary heroes, dream of heroic adventure in faraway lands. These dreams are not to be despised, for out of dreams achievements do come. But dreams cannot take the place of service to God in situations the children face every day.

So the challenge to mission must be extended in a form the child can respond to now. The cloud of witnesses surrounding the child points to ways in which God can be served.

The child's relationship to God is expressed in his behavior, his attitude toward people he knows, his loyalty to his own church and the opportunities it offers him to have a part in its outreach.

The child's relationship to God is expressed in friendly interest in the people of the world, in his resistance to prejudice and all attitudes that hurt and damage people.

The child's relationship to God is expressed in the invitation he extends to friends to join him in his church groups for no other reward than the satisfaction of finding that the friends who respond are glad they did.

The child's relationship to God makes him increasingly confident that God will care for him as God cares for others and give him the resources and help he needs when confronted with the painful and perplexing problems of growing up.

Although the child may not be able to express it in words, in ways that are appropriate for him he is a witness to the faith in which he is maturing. He is engaged in the Christian mission.

THE MISSION IMPERATIVE

At one of the most unlikely times in history the Christian church appeared on the scene and swept across the Eastern and Western worlds. It offered hope and love to a world sickened with despair and cruelty. It declared that there were beliefs that mattered and a God who cared. It said that men could be relieved of their intolerable feeling of guilt and sin by affirming their faith in Jesus Christ.

Two thousand years later, there are many who look upon the world of the twentieth century and wonder what progress mankind has achieved. There is still cruelty and despair and guilt. But Christian people know that the gospel has made a radical difference in the course of human history, and that it continues to offer the healing and hope men found in it long ago. Christian people also know that God still depends upon them to proclaim his gospel, to teach all men what Christ has taught to them.

Teachers of children in the church want boys and girls to be aware of how the gospel was carried to men and women in times past and what has happened because of the labors of these missionary representatives of God. This is one part of mission education.

But a still more important part of mission education is to help boys and girls who have accepted the gospel for themselves to know themselves as God's people, eager to witness in their own lives to the truth that they have found.

This is the mission imperative of the teacher and the imperative which the teacher earnestly hopes will be the possession of every child. There is only one reason for mission education: to help persons become involved in mission. It has a place in the children's division of the church because children, too, are called to be God's witnesses.

Bibliography

MATERIALS FOR LEADERS ON THE MISSION OF THE CHURCH

Johannes Blauw, *The Missionary Nature of the Church*. New York, Mc-Graw-Hill, 1962.

Malcolm Boyd, *Crisis in Communication*. New York, Doubleday, 1957.

Suzanne de Dietrich, *The Word with Power*. New York, Friendship Press, 1965.

Elisabeth D. Dodds, compiler, *Voices of Protest and Hope*. New York, Friendship Press, 1965.

Howard Grimes, *Realms of Our Calling*. New York, Friendship Press, 1965.

Bernard C. Ikeler and Stanley J. Rowland, Jr., *Mission as Decision*. New York, Friendship Press, 1965.

Tracey K. Jones, *Our Mission Today*. New York, World Outlook Press, 1963.

Hendrik Kraemer, *Communication of the Christian Faith*. Philadelphia, Westminster Press, 1956.

Martin E. Marty, *Babylon by Choice*. New York, Friendship Press, 1965.

——————, *The Improper Opinion*. Philadelphia, Westminster Press, 1961.

Jesse Jai McNeil, *The Preacher-Prophet in Mass Society*. Grand Rapids, William B. Eerdmans, 1961.

Donald G. Miller, *The Nature and Mission of the Church*. Richmond, John Knox Press, 1957.

Lesslie Newbigin, *The Household of God*. New York, Friendship Press, 1954.

D. T. Niles, *Upon the Earth.* New York, McGraw-Hill, 1962.

J. Allan Ranck, *Education for Mission.* New York, Friendship Press, 1961.

James E. Sellers, *The Outsider and the Word of God.* New York-Nashville, Abingdon Press, 1961.

Robert Spike, *In But Not of the World.* New York, Association Press, 1957.

Grace Storms Tower and Juanita P. Shacklett, Leadership Library. This Library includes: 1) *Growing Up in Mission,* the book you hold in your hand; 2) a filmstrip, *How John Grows Up in Mission;* 3) a parents' pamphlet, *Helping Your Child Grow Up in Mission;* and 4) *How to Use Your Leadership Library.* New York, Friendship Press, 1966.

George W. Webber, *The Congregation in Mission.* New York-Nashville, Abingdon, 1964.

BOOKS FOR CHILDREN ON THE MISSION OF THE CHURCH

Henry M. Bullock and Edward C. Peterson, editors, *Young Readers Bible.* Nashville, A. J. Holman Co. for Cokesbury, 1965.

Lulu Hathaway and Margaret Heppe, *They Lived Their Love.* New York, Friendship Press, 1965.

Mary Alice Jones, *God's Church Is Everywhere.* New York, Friendship Press, 1965.

Living as a Christian, compiled by Mildred Schell. New York, Friendship Press, 1965.

The *Little Playmate Books,* Sets I, II, and III. New York, Friendship Press.

World Friends Picture Albums, *The World's Children in Pictures* Series, and *Around the World* Picture Books. New York, Friendship Press.

BOOKS ON TEACHING-LEARNING ACTIVITIES

Elizabeth Allstrom, *Let's Play a Story.* New York, Friendship Press, 1957.

Dorothy LaCroix Hill, *The Church Teaches Nines to Twelves.* New York-Nashville, Abingdon, 1964.

Mary Alice Jones, *The Christian Faith Speaks to Children.* New York-Nashville, Abingdon, 1965.

Armilda B. Keiser, *Here's How and When.* New York, Friendship Press, 1960.

Nina Millen, *Children's Games from Many Lands.* New York, Friendship Press, revised 1965.

————, *Children's Festivals from Many Lands.* New York, Friendship Press, 1964.

Gertrude Priester, *Teaching Primary Children in the Church.* Philadelphia, Westminster Press, 1964.

Edith Lovell Thomas, *The Whole World Singing.* New York, Friendship Press, 1950.

HELPFUL AGENCIES

Write for catalogs listing available materials.

Association for Childhood Education International, 3615 Wisconsin Avenue, N.W., Washington, D. C.   20016.

Bank Street College Publications, 69 Bank Street, New York, N. Y.   10014.

B'nai Brith, 315 Lexington Avenue, New York, N. Y.   10016.

Child Study Association, 9 East 89th Street, New York, N. Y.   10028.

Children's Bureau, U. S. Department of Health, Education, and Welfare, Washington, D. C.   20025.

National Association for Mental Health, 10 Columbus Circle, New York, N. Y.   10019.

National Council of Churches of Christ, Department of Publication Services—Marketing and Promotion, 475 Riverside Drive, New York, N. Y. 10027.

National Education Association, 1201 Sixteenth Street, N.W., Washington, D. C.   20006.

Science Research Associates, 259 East Erie Street, Chicago, Ill.   60611.

World Council of Christian Education, 475 Riverside Drive, New York, N. Y.   10027.

Your denominational mission board and bookstores will be glad to supply you with listings of mission study materials, including recommended audio-visuals, recordings, and maps.

A WORD ABOUT THE FORMAT

Type: Times Roman 11 point leaded 2 points
Manufactured by: Sowers Printing Company, Lebanon, Pa.
Jackets and paper covers by: Affiliated Lithographers, Inc., New York
Text paper: Crestopake Text Vellum Finish
Typographic design by: Margery W. Smith
Binding design by: Louise E. Jefferson

PICTURE CREDITS

Page 12, photo by Heff Heisler
Page 52, photo by Jerry Spearman
Pages 82 and 158, photos by Bill Anderson